" *Consider the lilies of the field ....* "

from Maria, ——
for one of the nicest people
I've ever met ——

Josie ——

Knebworth . Summer 1987

The
Frampton Flora

I dedicate this book to the memory of my husband Peter Frazer Sinclair Clifford to whom these paintings meant so much.

Henriette Clifford, Frampton Court, 1985.

Count no men poor who have the stars above,
The peace and quietude of evening hours
And in their hearts that rarest gift of love
And in their garden — flowers.

Evelyn St Leger

The
Frampton Flora

Richard Mabey

The original suggestion for *The Frampton Flora* came from
Henriette and Peter Clifford of Frampton Court. All those concerned
with the preparation and production of the book thank them for
their encouragement. Others whose help is gratefully acknowledged
include Rollo and Janie Clifford of Frampton Manor, Sheila Clifford of
Wishanger, Gerda Barlow of Stancombe Park, Howard Beard, who
produced more information about the Clifford family, Dr Gordon
McGlone of the Gloucestershire Trust for Nature Conservation,
Brigadier Sparrow, John Workman, and the staff of the
Gloucestershire Record Office.

First published in Great Britain in 1985 by Century Publishing Co. Ltd.,
Portland House, 12-13 Greek Street, London W1V 5LE

The Frampton Flora was conceived, edited and designed by
Thames Head Limited, Avening, Tetbury, Gloucestershire, Great Britain

Editor	*Art editor*	*Designers*	*Co-ordinator*
Sandra Raphael	Tracey Arnold	Barry Chadwick	Marilyn Scott
		Nick Allen	

Typesetting by SP Typesetting, Birmingham

Reproduction by Redsend Limited, Birmingham

Printed in Great Britain by Purnell & Sons (Book Production) Bristol

Mabey, Richard
    The Frampton flora
    1. Wild flowers — England — Frampton on Severn
    (Gloucestershire) — Pictorial works
    I. Title
    582.13 '09424' 19   QK306

ISBN 0 7126 0859 1

Contents

Introduction

In 1837, the year a headstrong nineteen-year-old called Victoria Mary acceded to the English throne, a group of women in a remote corner of Gloucestershire began their own contribution to an era that was to become a byword for industriousness. There were at least eight of them, all members of the Clifford family of Frampton on Severn, and over the next twelve years they succeeded in making a collection of original paintings of nearly half the wild flowers of their native parish. These portraits, and a smaller number of illustrations of garden flowers, make up this *Frampton Flora*.

At face value it does not sound a very ambitious undertaking. Yet, in an age which put such a high premium on individual enterprise and female othodoxy, the paintings demonstrate a remarkable combination of collective effort and idosyncratic personal talent. They can stand comparison with the very best amateur work of this period of prolific botanical illustration. They are bold, exactly observed, beautifully and skilfully executed. Even the indifferent pictures (and there are a number of these) contain nothing mawkish or sentimental and make no wilful attempts to prettify their subjects. Where more orthodox Victorian amateurs reduced flower-painting to an exercise in trivial embroidery or extravagant self-expression, these women concentrated exclusively on their subjects, which, as a result, appear as unquestionably living plants, springing rough and ready from the earth. And as if to emphasize where the focus of attention properly lies, less than a fifth of the paintings are signed or accredited. Even when the identity of a particular artist is obvious from the style, the painting has often been captioned by one of the other women. One striking study of orchids (see page 91) actually contains the work of two different artists, with the species added last intimately interwoven, as if it were behind the first.

When the paintings were rediscovered in 1982, the colours were so bright that they can scarcely have seen the light since they were first made. They had been stitched up in scrap-books and confined to an attic at Frampton Court, plainly regarded as of no special account. That isn't surprising, for in the first half of the nineteenth century flower-painting was as conventional a domestic skill for ladies of a certain social position as cordon bleu cooking is today. Even collections as accomplished as this cannot, by themselves, be taken as signs of early feminist stirrings. There is certainly nothing here to suggest a determined attempt to confront the still largely masculine scientific world on its own terms, no planned thoroughness in the coverage, no hint of a desire for publication, and nothing approaching the enterprise of Anne Pratt, the grocer's daughter from Chatham, who during the same period painted and wrote five famous volumes covering the entire British flora.

Sweet violet, Viola odorata, *May 6th, 1839. Charlotte Clifford*

But if it showed no aggressive ambition, the Cliffords' work had the more appealing virtues of collaboration and that quiet professionalism that has become the hallmark of amateur natural history. The more one studies this collection as a whole, and the evidence about how it was produced, the more probable it seems that the women worked as a team, planning their subjects in advance (virtually no species are repeated in the surviving pictures), making expeditions together, comparing finished work and selecting the best for preservation.

The project even has echoes of folk art in its sense of being not just a close family activity but a communal exploration of the way the home grounds were marked out by their seasonable growths. Ronald Blythe, writing of his Suffolk boyhood, remembers a similar recognition of the links between plants and places persisting until the Second World War: 'Village people of all ages saw them as a form of permanent geography, by which the distances of Sunday walks could be measured, or where tea or love could be made.'* Perhaps not love for these mostly single women, but tea and Sunday walks most certainly, and probably, even if half-consciously, that sense of the 'permanent geography' of their ancestral territory.

The Cliffords had first come to Frampton nearly eight hundred years before, when Drogo fitz Pons, a Norman nobleman who had been with William the Conqueror during the invasion of England, was given the manor as a reward for his services. Drogo died without heirs, and it was his grandson Walter, from Clifford in Herefordshire, who brought the present family name to Gloucestershire.

* *From the Headlands,* London, 1982

Sweet violet, Viola odorata, *1835 Charlotte Anne Purnell*

The area in which the Cliffords lived and painted.

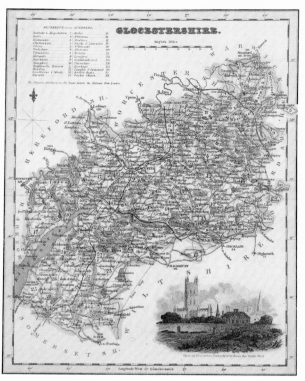

Map kindly reproduced from Gloucester Records Office

They could hardly have found themselves a more prosperous or congenial seat. It lay on the rich alluvial soil of the Severn Vale, with Gloucester just ten miles to the north and the then thriving ports of the river Severn within easy reach to the west. There was ample building material close at hand too. Gravel for road-mending lay under the village itself; there was clay for brick-making on the marshes and limestone on the Cotswold scarp, a few miles to the east. While they remained lords of the manor, the Cliffords were able to consolidate their position in Frampton. They built cottages, a lodge, and a substantial mansion, Frampton Court, across the green from the manor-house itself. They farmed extensive lands around the village, and, as was the custom among richer landowners, made occasional penitential gifts to the priories at Malvern and Godstow.

Beyond the round of the agricultural year, and occasional inundations by the Severn, Frampton and the Cliffords had relatively uneventful histories. In the twelfth century there was a minor scandal when Rosamond Clifford (died 1177) became Henry II's mistress. But the general opinion was that she had been badly used, and in the 1650s Frampton's village green began to be called Rosamond's Green in her memory. Earlier in the seventeenth century the manor itself passed out of the family when a female heir married, and the manorial rights were subsequently sold outright to the Alderman of Bristol. A hundred years later the original Frampton Court burned down and was rebuilt as the present house.

Through all these occasional reverses in their fortunes, the Cliffords showed a resolute determination to survive. Even when they lost both manor and manor-house they continued to live in all the family's other properties in the village. And when the direct line of descent was broken in the late seventeenth century by a sequence of unmarried sons and female heirs, the impressive antiquity of the family seemed enough to persuade an outsider to seek royal permission to resurrect its name.

So, in 1801, Nathaniel Winchombe, an in-law five generations removed from the last person to bear the name Clifford in Frampton, became Nathaniel Clifford, and his son Henry Clifford became Henry Clifford Clifford. It was the female children of Henry's marriage to Mary Packer of Painswick who began the dynasty of women responsible for the paintings. It underlines still more the resilience and parochial loyalties of the family that almost all of them, even when married, were still to be found occupying traditional Clifford houses in Frampton. In the 1851 census, for instance, the households were recorded as follows. At Frampton Court itself, Henry Clifford Clifford, then 65 years old and a widower for eleven years, his five unmarried daughters (Elizabeth, aged 42; Mary Anne, 37; Charlotte, 36; Catherine, 30; and Constance, 24), one of his five surviving sons, plus seven servants. At the cottage next door were Henry's two unmarried sisters, Catherine Elizabeth, 66, and Rosamond, 57, and two female servants. The biggest clutch was at Frampton Lodge where Henry's eldest son, another Henry, had set up house with his wife Marianne (previously M. Phelps). She was 34 years old at the time and already had two daughters and four sons, with a young Swiss governess and two young nursery-maids to care for them. A footman, a cook and a housemaid made up the complement.

The most fascinating house was Stancombe Park near Stinchcombe, about eight miles to the south of Frampton. Here at the very foot of the Cotswolds, set in exquisitely landscaped grounds and surrounded by wilder beechwoods and limestone downs, Henry's sister Charlotte Anne (born 1791) lived with her husband Purnell Bransby Purnell.

Stancombe was a favourite botanizing haunt for the whole family, and many of the choicest plants in this collection, especially the orchids, were found and painted there.

It is impossible to guess why so very few of these two generations of Clifford women married; but the consequence was that they were relatively free of responsibilities and had an abundance of free time to spend in fashionable pastimes like needlework, archery and music, as well as painting. Since the paintings themselves were rediscovered a number of mementoes of this period have re-emerged to help build up a picture of the context in which they were produced. The most striking impression they give is of the extent to which drawings and paintings were used as a means of preserving family memories and records. They were the exact contemporary equivalent of snapshots. There are paintings of picnics, archery contests, school outings, Christmas parties, favourite servants, paintings of each other and even paintings of painting.

The Clifford family tree 1757 - 1910

Few of these have anything like the quality of the flower illustrations, and it is plain that their role was not as works of art but documentary records. They were a kind of visual gossip. Who sat next to whom? What did they wear? What did they do? These were the questions these scrap-book pages had to answer and they often did so with a cartoonist's wit that more than makes up for their lack of technique. One of the most ambitious, though floundering in the problems of perspective presented by a wide open-air scene, is of an outing by the Severn in July 1843. A row of Clifford women sit on a bench, gazing out at a sailing-ship passing up the river. Their faces seem quite wilfully obscured by their Quaker bonnets, but all their names are listed, left to right, at the foot of the painting. The men wear heavy black coats and stove-pipe hats, and in the background one of them, ominously stoking up a muzzle-loader, is confronting a herd of pigs advancing on the picnic baskets.

But there are more obviously artistic records too, including a series of small sketches make by Catherine Clifford in the 1860s of almost all the houses in Frampton, and of the women's haunts near Stinchcombe and the muddy flats of the Severn. They are largely done in ink, pencil and wash, and have the kind of meticulous attention to scale and detail (including notes on the occupants of each property) that one would expect from modern postcards.

Other documents which have proved useful in assembling this book are some fragments of a journal, consisting chiefly of rather pious quotations, and a domestic recipe book dating from the 1820s and written in Rosamond's hand. This is a compilation of remedies (chiefly for coughs and rheumatism; the dank Severn Vale obviously exacted its toll) culled from friends, neighbours and books, and making extensive use of both wild and garden herbs.

The flower paintings, therefore, were in one sense just an extension of a routine family custom, and of a way of life which involved a good deal of activity out in the country. What makes them special is, first, their high artistic quality, and second, the social significance botany was beginning to assume in women's lives.

Women had long had a special relationship with flowering plants. In both Celtic and Anglo-Saxon society, for instance, they had responsibility for growing and using curative herbs. In Tudor England they would generally tend the plants in gardens while men cultivated those in the fields. But in none of these periods would the facile suggestion have been made that it was a shared delicacy that made females and flowers such appropriate companions. Yet this was the assumption that underlay even the best intentioned attempts to make botany a useful domestic pastime in the eighteenth century. When Thomas Martyn, Professor of Botany at Cambridge, published his translation of and additions to Rousseau's *Letters on the Elements of Botany Addressed to Ladies*, his personal vision of the value of botany for ladies is unequivocally stated in his preface. He was convinced 'that at all times of life the study of nature abates the taste for frivolous amusements, prevents the tumult of passions and provides the mind with a nourishment which is salutary by filling it with an object most worthy of its contemplation.' He dedicated the book to those obviously superior blooms, 'The Ladies of Great Britain, no less eminent for their elegant and useful accomplishments than admired for the beauty of their persons.'

In the period after its publication in 1785 the book was a best-seller, especially in country seats, where, presumably, there were few alternative antidotes to 'the tumult of passions', and over the next fifty years the advantages of botany as a respectable, even devout, form of occupational therapy were vigorously promoted. There was nothing wrong with this at all, except that it was clearly understood that the matter should go no further. As late as the mid-1850s, the Scottish geologist and stonemason, Hugh Miller, could write to his fiancée: 'O my own Lydia, be careful of yourself. Take little thought and much exercise. Read for amusement only. Set yourself to make a collection of shells, or butterflies, or plants. Do anything that will have interest enough to amuse you without requiring so much attention as to fatigue.' (This, needless to say, was a rather

The Clifford clan, on an expedition to the River Severn, July 1843.

different standard from the one Miller set himself, and he would regularly walk miles to dig for thought-provoking fossils after a hard day's work in the quarries.)

Yet if the fashionable regarded the study of botany as the acquisition of a demanding yet decorous social grace (plenty of intricate steps but strictly no improvisation) many women found that they could not remain dilettantes in its pursuit. The raw material was intrinsically too fascinating and challenging. Living plants are not like samplers. They confront anyone with an open mind with the reality of growth and decay. They trigger curiosity about form and function and the relationships of species one with another. In the eighteenth and nineteenth centuries they also faced even the most elementary student with real-life models of the Linnaean sexual system for the classification of plants. Since this was the basis of the tidy formalism that was regarded as one of botany's major educational virtues, there was some embarrassment when Linnaeus's avid attempts to explain his system proved to have all the hilarious bawdiness of a bedroom farce. Searching for a popular metaphor to explain the arrangement of stamens and pistils inside the flower, Linnaeus hit upon the marriage couch, with the result that various plant families were described as, for instance 'Diandria: Two husbands in the same marriage', or even more scandalously 'Polyandria: Twenty males or more in the same bed with the female'.

But it was not so much this or that individual issue which was important as the fact that botany could not help but provide some intellectual challenge. It provided a respectable avenue for women to get out of the house, to think, talk and work. It is no coincidence that the eighteenth-and nineteenth-century salon tradition had intimate connections with the natural sciences. As early as the 1750s groups of progressive women (dubbed 'petticoteries' by Horace Walpole) had turned the convention of drawing-room chit-chat on its head by establishing a wide-ranging series of discussion groups, or conversazioni. 'Such women,' David Elliston Allen has suggested, 'made learning fashionable for the hitherto unlearned sex; and it is pleasant to recall that the name "bluestocking", which was hurled at them and stuck, derived from the

A picnic in a woodland glade. But who is painting the painters?

eccentric garb in which one of their prominent friends, Benjamin Stillingfleet, regularly came to the parties to discourse (we may presume) on botany, and explain to them the delightful parlour-game invented by Linnaeus.'

By the close of the eighteenth century, when the older generation of Clifford painters was growing up, these two faces of botany - the diversionary and the studious - had reached a compromise in the enthusiasm for painting flowers. It was the era of supreme illustrators like Redouté and the Bauer brothers, and over the next few decades there was a flood of books designed to reveal the tricks of their trade to leisured women. Mary Lawrance published *Sketches of Flowers from Nature* in 1801 to help beginners acquire 'that Ultimatum of the Art ... a natural Appearance'. Peter Henderson's *The Seasons, or Flower Garden ... with a Treatise or General Instruction for Painting* appeared in 1806 and George Brookshaw's *Every Lady her Own Drawing Master* (sic) in 1818. In 1831 the distinguished gardener and botanist John Loudon added his personal seal of approval by writing: 'To be able to draw Flowers botanically,... is one of the most useful accomplishments of your ladies of leisure, living in the country.' That, of course, was a perfect description of the women of Frampton Court and Stancombe Park, and there can be little doubt that they owned, or had seen, at least some of these books.

What is striking is the extent to which, right from the outset, the women ignored much of their teaching. Most of these books were still dominated by the idea of the beneficial discipline of flower-painting. They frequently recommended copying from (or colouring in) their own plates, and concentrated above all else on plant anatomy; 'to be able to draw Flowers botanically,' as Loudon had written, and added, by way of explanation 'that is, with the characteristics by which varieties and subvarieties are prominent'. When James Sowerby, one of the most distinguished botanists of his day and illustrator of the definitive *English Botany* (1790-1814) published *A Botanical Drawing-Book* ('to facilitate Botanical Studies and blend Amusement with Improvement'), only the very last page has any details at all about the technique of painting. The remainder is exclusively concerned with the variety of forms of petals, fruits and leaves to be found in the plant world.

There is, in contrast, little evidence of overt copying in the Cliffords' work. Out of nearly three hundred surviving paintings only seventeen have obviously been based on published illustrations. The models appear to be confined to two sources: the second edition of Smith and Sowerby's *English Botany* and William Baxter's *British Phaenogamous Botany* (1834-43). (Much of Baxter's work had in fact been published as a popular monthly serial with the title of *British Flowering Plants*, and a set of copies of this part-work still survives among the remnants of Marianne Clifford's library. It is annotated in her hand, and was probably one of the family's chief reference works.) There is no clear link between the copies. Most are of species, such as water soldier, chickweed wintergreen and water germander, that do not occur wild in Gloucestershire. A few of the remainder have been included in the following pages, where it seems possible that they had also been seen in the field.

Nor did the Cliffords follow the practice developed among scientific illustrators of portraying flowers with their identifying parts dissected and displayed. Their illustrations are of whole plants and there is every reason to believe that the vast majority were painted from life, using specimens found in the close vicinity of their home villages. Indeed, many of the handwritten captions are precise about both the date of the paintings and the site where the plant was found. Only three locations outside the Frampton-Stinchcombe area are specified: a mountain pansy painted 'From the Caradoc Hill Shropshire' (not included here); a hound's-tongue from Clevedon, on the banks of the Severn some thirty miles south of Frampton; and six relatively common species from 'Leamington', all painted during the summer of 1845. (It isn't clear whether this is Leamington in Warwickshire or a mis-spelling of Lemington in Somerset, where Henry Clifford's butler was born; but in any case all six species were common in Frampton itself.)

We can picture the women setting out on their sketching expeditions, probably in groups, and accompanied by brothers, friends and servants. To judge from the species they found, they covered their home territory exhaustively, trekking across fields and damp meadows, up the steep, grazed slopes of the Cotswolds and into the heart of the woods. They would have had to follow their own instincts as to where the best sites were, as no kind of guide existed to local vegetation. J.L. Knapp's study of the natural history of Alveston (north of Bristol), the *Journal of a Naturalist*, had been published in 1829 and contained some notes on the vegetation of the Severn Vale, but a systematic mapping of the county's flora did not really begin until the same year the Cliffords began work. In 1837, Professor J.J. Buckman began publishing lists of local plants in the *Cheltenham Magazine*, and seven years later compiled what was to be the county's earliest local flora, *A Botanical Guide to the Environs of Cheltenham*.

Some of the species found by the Cliffords were almost certainly sketched in the field, and one of the more endearing of the family album drawings shows just such a working picnic in progress. It is taking place in what appears to be a woodland glade. There are seven picnickers present, including one untraceable male companion, sitting with an enigmatic smile on his face and doing absolutely nothing. John, the youngest son, is deep in a book under the shade of a rustic straw hat. Next to him is a friend Julia, knitting or lace-making. Charlotte is embroidering, Harriet (untraceable, though a Harriet Bennet was a kitchen-maid at Frampton Court) is playing a dulcimer, and Catherine is sketching or painting on a pad on her lap. As seemed to be their custom, all the women are wearing bonnets and heavy-duty shawls. The shooting jackets and 'sensible boots' recommended by Miss Plues in her best-seller, *Rambles in Search of Wildflowers* (1863), are still some way away, but not, obviously, the active and inquisitive life she championed for young women.

The paintings were probably finished off at home, perhaps in the sunlit orangery overlooking the ornamental canal at Frampton Court, where the sisters often took tea. The artists probably composed the final paintings using a combination of field sketches and picked (and maybe pressed) specimens for reference. It is doubtful if they ever painted-in their sketches, for one of the remarkable features of the collection is the absence of any visible pencil work. Even the most delicate leaves and petals are outlined purely by means of skilled brushwork. The women worked exclusively in water-colours, using washes most of the time and reserving concentrated body-colour for the brighter blooms. The clarity of the paintings was helped by the high quality of their paper, and a particular favourite was a thick Bristol board, priced with a pencilled tuppence in the corner of the sheet.

Family portraits: left: Catherine Clifford right: Charlotte Clifford

When each painting was complete it was usually captioned (sometimes rather scrappily) in ink. The plant's Linnaean family and conventional English and Latin names were given, and often the date. Sometimes a location (presumably where the specimen was found) was added and, exceptionally, the artist's initials.

A considerable number of paintings, chiefly of garden flowers, remained as loose sheets. But the majority - just over two hundred, in fact - survived mounted in three small, leather-bound albums. It is impossible to know exactly what the women (or woman) responsible were hoping to achieve by this method of organizing their illustrations, but a number of clues suggest it may have been a kind of family flora. The mounted illustrations are all of wild and, with a very few exceptions, local species, and inside each scrap-book they have been arranged according to their Linnaean classification, but that is about as far as strict botanical considerations appear to go. There has been no attempt to include all the members of one family in a single book or to arrange them according to habitat or time of painting.

It seems more likely that the arrangement reflects connections between particular paintings and particular Clifford women. The fly-leaf of the first album, for instance, carries the names 'Catherine Clifford, 1865', and 'Rosamond Clifford, 1842', and the second Mary Anne Clifford's name. But do these inscriptions refer to authorship or ownership? It is hard to believe that the variety of styles in the individual albums belong to only one or two artists. The handwriting in the captions is even more changeable, and it looks as if these were occasionally completed by a second or even third party. And whoever's rather shaky hand it was that added Catherine Elizabeth's initials (CEC) to a number of paintings in all three books, it was not often the same one that wrote their captions.

My own view is that since the main impetus behind the project seemed to be a desire for collaborative rather than individual achievement, it is as well to allow the authorship of most of the individual paintings to remain vague. But there are enough exceptions - where paintings have been initialled or where a strong personal style shows through - to build up a general picture of the contributions made by various members of the family. It looks as if at least eight took some part in the painting. Of the younger generation, Catherine seems to have done a good deal of work for the family albums, and may be responsible for many of the more run-of-the-mill paintings. Her sister Charlotte's signature appears against a number of precise and accomplished paintings, and Mary Anne's against just one (hound's-tongue, on page 107). But because of the similarity in style (chiefly the bold, sweeping leaf-work) between this painting and several in the original album which bears her name, I have taken the liberty of suggesting Mary Anne as the artist of a few unsigned pictures.

The older generation, the aunts at Frampton Cottage and Stancombe, were more liberal with their signatures. Rosamond contributed some fine, painstaking, garden-flower portraits. Catherine Elizabeth's highly characteristic work is chiefly of the flowering tops of plants - almost as if they had been snipped off - with the stalk given a slight, serpentine wave (see, for instance, wild basil, on page 110).

Marianne Clifford in widow's weeds, January 30th 1864

A fond, if none too flattering, sketch of one of the Frampton Court servants, probably Frances Read, the housekeeper

But it is Charlotte Anne Purnell's (CAP) paintings that are the outstanding examples in the collection. Her work unites the best of the styles which dominated the world of flower-painting in the first half of the nineteenth century - the exact, anatomical work of Sowerby, John Curtis, and the other illustrators of the famous *Botanical Magazine*; and the richer, more opulent, though no less precise work following Continental painters like Ehret and Redouté. But Charlotte Anne had many uniquely personal gifts, not least a remarkable ability to design a plant on the page without destroying its natural effect, and a characteristically soft range of colours. (Compare, for instance, her painting of sweet violet with Charlotte Clifford's, on page 7.)

*

Between them, the Cliffords painted a comprehensive picture of the vegetation of their home countryside. And because this landscape was so diverse, enabling them to move from limestone hills a thousand feet high through woods, downs, farmland and fen, to reach tidal river and salt-marsh in less than five miles, the *Frampton Flora* is also a fair portrait of the state of lowland England's flora in the middle of the nineteenth century.

But just as significant as what the Cliffords included may be what they left out. Some of the omissions may be purely technical. They did not portray many white flowers, for example, perhaps because the quality of white paints was still rather poor. They attempted only one of the fiddling small-flowered umbellifers (see shepherd's needle on page 151). But some absentees are less explicable. Why, for instance, are there so few of the small herbs - thyme, marjoram, salad burnet - that dominate the limestone downs at Stinchcombe? Why no teasel, a dramatic painter's flower if ever there was one, and not only common in the ditches round Frampton, but actually (in one form) grown as a crop there in the mid-nineteenth century?

To suggest that there is a pattern behind the selection would be to overestimate the evidence. But I think there was a tendency, which was to concentrate on the familiar, more humdrum flowers in the lanes and fields round Frampton and on the rarer, more glamorous species in the wilder country round Stinchcombe. Was this their personal reflection of the Victorian spirit, with its twin passions for domesticity and expansiveness?

That much, perhaps, is speculation. But the Frampton collection is, by any standards, an expression both of parochial loyalties and of a lively curiosity, and it is these two elements that I have tried to bring out in the pages that follow. I have arranged the species according to the habitats in which they would have been found, and confined the text to notes on those local characteristics - customs, namings, landscapes - that would have affected the Cliffords most directly. In this way I think that we can look across the hundred-and-fifty years (it is only five generations after all) that separate us from the Clifford women, and see more clearly not only what has changed in our countryside but to what degree our responses to it have remained the same.

Plan of the Flora

I have arranged the paintings into sections corresponding to habitat types. Although this inevitably means a certain arbitrariness about where to place some of the commoner species, I feel it does give a better sense of how and where the paintings were made, and of the changes in the local flora over the past century-and-a-half.

The illustrations accompanying the introductions in these sections are mostly from Catherine Clifford's village sketch-book (see page 10).

The order in which the species are placed inside each section (except the one on Gardens) follows that in the Clapham, Tutin and Warburg *Flora of the British Isles*, though occasionally pictures are placed out of order to emphasize points about local ecology or painting style.

The English and Latin names are not those used by the Cliffords, but follow *English Names of Wild Flowers*, by J.G. Dony and others.

The date, site and signature are taken, when they appear, from the captions on the original paintings, with the abbreviations expanded to painters' names as follows:

MAC - Mary Anne Clifford
CC - Charlotte Clifford
RC - Rosamond Clifford
CEC - Catherine Elizabeth Clifford
CAP - Charlotte Anne Purnell
HP - probably Helen Purnell, Charlotte Anne's daughter, born in 1825.

Where names are given in brackets the paintings have not been signed, but the painter deduced from stylistic points.

The distribution notes refer to current frequency and favoured habitats. Where no mention is made of the frequency, the species can be assumed to be common and widespread then and now. Except where stated, these notes refer to the occurrence of species nationally as well as locally.

In the case of more restricted species, a fuller note on their local distribution in the vicinity of Frampton and Stinchcombe is given.

Authorities for distribution are Clapham, Tutin and Warburg's *Flora of the British Isles*, Perring and Walters's *Atlas of the British Flora*, and the *Flora of Gloucestershire*, by Riddelsdell and others. Local names are based on this flora, Geoffrey Grigson's *The Englishman's Flora* and Britten and Holland's *Dictionary of English Plant-names*.

An early photograph of Frampton Court, with an archery contest in progress on the lawn

May 8th 1867

Frampton Court from the

The Home Ground

If the Clifford women had been less naturally inquisitive they could have painted maybe a third of all the species in this book without ever leaving the grounds of their family home. Frampton Court was then, as now, a complex working estate. There were orchards, walled gardens, stables, and a vast area of grazed parkland. There was an ornamental Dutch canal, connected by an underground channel to the ponds on Rosamond's Green.

But neither Frampton nor its flora were in a static state. As the fortunes of the estate waxed and waned, scrub and weeds advanced and were beaten back. Coaches coming up the majestic carriageways would bring foreign seeds as well as exotic human visitors. And along them also travelled the Clifford artists, returning from trips with slips of plants to sketch and perhaps set down in the garden.

Their most convenient port of call was Rosamond's Green, which lay just a hundred yards beyond the house. Since this had been drained by their grandfather it had become a much more pleasant and accessible area. There were geese on the ponds and tethered horses grazing among the cowslips and birdsfoot trefoil. The Cliffords made many sketches of the green and its surroundings, and it is clear that by the mid-nineteenth century, it had turned into a convivial meeting-place for the villagers as well as for their animals.

Meadow buttercup
Ranunculus acris
June 20th 1850
Meadows, waysides

Bulbous buttercup
Ranunculus bulbosus
May 28th 1846, Frampton Park
Meadows, waysides

Polyandria Polygynia
Ranunculus Repens Creeping Crowfoot
June 1st 1846 Frampton

Creeping buttercup
Ranunculus repens
June 1846, Frampton
Waysides, damp disturbed ground

Ranunculus. Ficaria Pilewort Crowfoot
March 23— 1840
Polyandria Polygynia

All yellow-flowered members of the buttercup family share a curious collection of local names in Gloucestershire, including gold knops or knobs and crazy.

Lesser celandine
Ranunculus ficaria
March 23rd 1840
Woods, damp shady places

Chelidonium Majus Common Celandine
Polyandria Monogynia.

Greater celandine is not related to its lesser namesake, but is a member of the poppy family, hence the latex (orange in this species) which exudes when the stem or leaves are broken. This is bitter and mildly corrosive, and was widely used for cauterizing warts, though without much success. The plant's local names throughout western England refer to this ancient medicinal use. Kill-wart has been recorded in Devon, wart-plant in Somerset and wartwort in Gloucestershire.

It was West Country settlers who first took the plant to the United States and with it an even earlier herbal name: swallow wort. This recalled the classical myth that swallows used the juice to cleanse their nestlings' eyes, and even to restore their sight if they had been injured. Later herbalists poured scorn on this story, but were not slow to recommend the acrid latex, which 'consumeth awaie slimie things that cleave about the ball of the eie', according to John Gerard.

Greater celandine
Chelidonium majus
Frequent in dry, waste places,
especially close to habitation

Tetradynamia Siliquosa
Cardamine Pratensis Common Lady's Smock

May 9th 1843

Local names: ach, corrupted to headache, cuckoos, and a number of splendidly saucy, punning variations on the smock theme, including smell-smock and smick-smock (to smicker was to gaze amorously).

Cuckoo flower or Lady's smock
Cardamine pratensis
May 9th 1843
Damp grassland, riversides

A beautifully constructed painting, given a perfect balance by a few lightly drawn yellowing leaves at the base. It has the characteristic sharpness of line and layout of Charlotte Clifford's work.

Tetradynamia Siliquosa
Cardamine Hirsuta
Hairy Ladies Smock
November 16th 1844   CC

Hairy bittercress
Cardamine hirsuta
November 16th 1844
Gardens, cultivated fields and waste
ground

Thlaspi Bursa-pastoris
Shepherd's Purse Mithridate Mustard
Tetradynamia Siliculosa
October 31st 1844 –

Local name: mother's heart
(derived from the shape of the seed cases, as is the common English name).

Shepherd's purse
Capsella bursa-pastoris
October 31st 1844
Cultivated and waste ground

Tetradynamia Siliquosa.
Erysimum Alliaria

Garlick Hedge Mustard
or
Jack by the Hedge
May 13th 1848

Garlic mustard or Jack-by-the-hedge
Alliaria petiolata
May 13th 1848
Waysides, woods

Monodelphia Polyandria
Malva rotundifolia
Dwarf Mallow   July 1843

Decandria Trigynia   April 1843
Stellaria Media   Common Chickweed Stitchwort

Chickweed
Stellaria media
April 1843
Cultivated and waste ground

Dwarf mallow
Malva neglecta
July 1843
Waste ground and waysides

Monadelphia Polyandria

Malva Sylvestris Common Mallow

An impressively elegant and accurate picture, catching both the range of shadings of the flower petals and their delicate, porcelain texture.

Common mallow
Malva sylvestris
Waste ground and waysides

Monodelphia Decandria
Geranium Molle Dove's foot Cranesbill
May 21st 1846 Frampton Green

Geranium Robertianum Monadelphia Decandria
Stinking Cranesbill
Stancombe June 1838

Local names include London pink, wild pink, red robin, small robin's eye. The name used to label the painting, stinking cranesbill, refers to the rank, mousy smell of the crushed leaves.

Dove's-foot cranesbill
Geranium molle
May 21st 1846, Frampton Green
Fields, waysides and waste places
Still quite common on Frampton Green

Herb Robert
Geranium robertianum
June 1838, Stancombe
Woods, waysides and shady waste places

Local names: butter and eggs, crowfeet, eggs and bacon, hen-and-chickens, pattens-and-clogs, shoes-and-stockings.

A good selection from the seventy-odd common names that have been recorded for this species around Britain, which show how affectionately and closely (and fancifully, some might say) people have observed the shape and colour of the flowers.

Common bird's-foot trefoil
Lotus corniculatus
Waysides, grassy places

Pale willow-herb
Epilobium roseum
August 14th 1848
Waste places

The Art of Drawing Leaves

Dioecia Pentandria
Humulus Lupulus
Common Hop Sept 2nd 1848

These paintings of four common climbing plants - three of which have the velvety leaf texture and superb sense of design of Charlotte Anne Purnell's work - suggest some acquaintance with the more naturalistic schools of medieval flower-painters and carvers. In the remarkable set of representational plant carvings in Southwell Minster in Nottinghamshire, hop and white bryony are among the leaves which appear most frequently in the decorative carvings on the tops of the columns. It seems to have been the symmetrical, many-fingered form of these leaves which attracted carvers, for the other species which are most frequently figured in ornamentation during this period are the vine, mulberry, oak, hawthorn and cinquefoil. The commonest leaf in the Southwell carvings is field maple, and the painting of this species on page 64 shows up these characteristics well, though they are not used there to any decorative effect.

Here the artists are echoing the medieval craftsmen, even if only unconsciously, in the flat, spiralling patterns of leaf-points and lobes.

Hop
Humulus lupulus
September 2nd 1848
A climbing plant of hedges and waste
places

Known as mandrake in parts of Gloucestershire and elsewhere because of its root. Gerard described this as 'very great and thicke, oftentimes as bigge as a mans legge, blackish without, and very clammie or slimy within; which being but scraped with a knife, or any other thing fit for that purpose, it seemeth to be a matter fit to spread upon cloth or leather in manner of a plaister or seare-cloth; which being so spread and used…taketh away blacke or blewe markes, all scarres and deformities of the skin, breaketh harde apostemes, draweth foorth splinters and broken bones, dissolveth congealed bloud; and being laid on and used upon the hippe or huckle bones, shoulders, armes, or any other part where there is great paine and ache, it taketh it away in short space.' It was probably as just such a poultice that the root was used locally as a horse medicine, though it must have been a rather risky remedy: both the roots and the scarlet berries contain powerful irritant poisons, which have caused severe gastro-enteritis in horses.

Black bryony
Tamus communis
July 4th 1846, Stancombe
(Charlotte Anne Purnell?)
Hedges, waste ground
A fairly common climber in hedges
and woods

Bryonia dioica. Red berried Brgony.
Monoecia Pentandria.

Stancombe, June 27ᵗʰ 1846.

White bryony
Bryonia dioica
June 27th 1846, Stancombe
(Charlotte Anne Purnell?)
Hedges, waste ground

Pentandria Monogynia.

Convolvulus Sepium — Great Bindweed.

Hedge bindweed
Calystegia sepium
August 20th 1840
(Charlotte Anne Purnell?)
Waste ground, hedgerows

Icosandria Polygynia
Potentilla Anserina Silverweed cinquefoil
July 1847

Icosandria Polygynia.
Potentilla Reptans.
Common creeping cinquefoil.—
C.A.P.

Creeping cinquefoil
Potentilla reptans
Waysides and waste places
Local name: five-finger-grass
The soft colours and elegantly sinuous
layout are typical of Charlotte Anne
Purnell's work

Silverweed
Potentilla anserina
July 1847
Fields, waysides, waste places
Local name: goose-grass

Class 12th Order 3rd Icosandria Polygynia

Rosa Canina Dog Rose

Dog rose
Rosa canina
Hedges, scrub, open woods

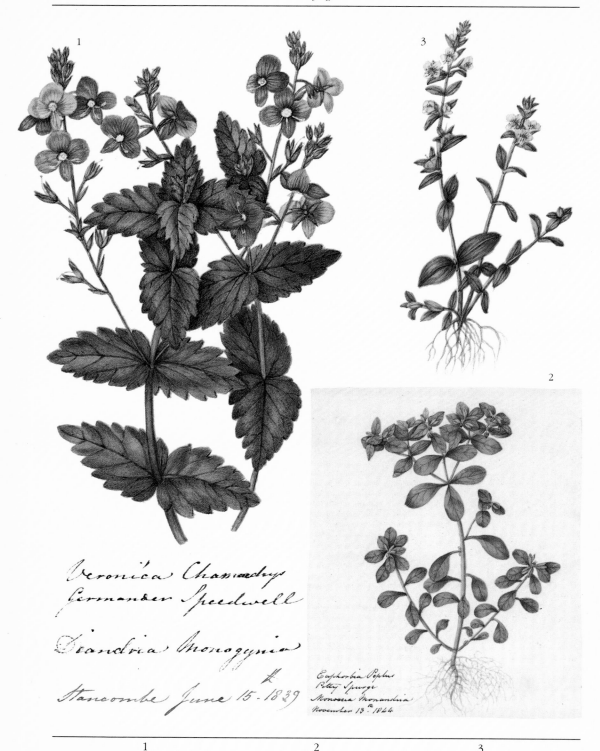

Veronica Chamaedrys
Germander Speedwell

Diandria Monogynia

Stancombe June 15 - 1839

Euphorbia Peplus
Petty Spurge
Monoecia Monandria
November 13 - 1844

1	2	3
Germander speedwell	**Petty spurge**	**Thyme-leaved speedwell**
Veronica chamaedrys	*Euphorbia peplus*	*Veronica serpyllifolia*
June 15th 1839, Stancombe	November 13th 1844	May 18th 1846, Frampton
Waysides, grassland, woods	Waste and cultivated ground	Waste and cultivated ground and
Local names: bird's-eye, cat's eyes		grassy places
(from the white pupil at the centre of		
the blue petals)		

Local name: ettle
In a remedy which is reminiscent of
sympathetic magic the Frampton domestic
recipe book recommends stinging nettle tea
as a cure for nettle-rash.

Monoecia Tetrandria
Urtica Dioica Great Nettle

1

Diandria Monogynia   April 1843
Veronica Hederifolia Ivy-leaved Speedwell

Tetrandria Monogynia
Parietaria Officinalis

*Blossom & Involucre
much magnified
seldom so perfect*

*Common Pellitory of the Wall
July 9th 1850*

1	2	3
Ivy-leaved speedwell	**Common nettle or stinging nettle**	**Pellitory-of-the-wall**
Veronica hederifolia	*Urtica dioica*	*Parietaria judaica*
April 1843	Waste ground, waysides	July 9th 1850
Disturbed and cultivated ground		Almost exclusively on old walls

Tedynamia Gymnospermia
Glechoma hederacea Common Ground Ivy May 2nd 1843

Local names: Gill, hay-maidens (probably hedge-maidens originally) and runaway Jack, a reference to its habit of ramping about damp and shady places in gardens and sometimes climbing up into shrubs.

Ground ivy
Glechome hederacea
May 2nd 1843
Woods, waysides

1

Didynamia Gymnospermia
Prunella Vulgaris Common Selfheal
Leamington July 26th 1845

2

Didynamia Gymnospermia
Ballota nigra Black Fetid Horehound
August 29th 1850

3

Lamium Purpureum
Red dead Nettle

April 27th 1839

Local names: fly-flowers, carpenter's herb
Selfheal was formerly recommended as a
wound-herb, perhaps because of the
suggestive 'signature' of a bill or reaping
hook in the upper lip of the flower. John
Gerard, who believed that a 'decoction of
Prunell made with wine or water, doth ioine
togither and make whole and sound all
wounds, both inward and outward,' lists its
English names as 'Carpenters Herbe…
Hookeheale, & Sicklewoort'. The first
persisted in Gloucestershire until this
century, perhaps because of the strong
wood-working tradition in the Cotswold
beechwoods.

1	2	3
Self-heal	**Black horehound**	**Red dead-nettle**
Prunella vulgaris	*Ballota nigra*	*Lamium purpureum*
July 26th 1845, Leamington	August 29th 1850	April 27th 1839
Waysides, grassy places	Waste ground, waysides	Waste and cultivated ground
		Recommended for making into
		poultices in the Frampton domestic
		recipe book

Tetrandria Monogynia
Plantago Major
Greater Plantain

June 24th 1850

Greater plantain
Plantago major
June 24th 1850
Disturbed, compacted and bare
ground

Ribwort and hoary plantain share the intriguing local names of fireweed and fireleaves. The origin of these is not certain, but it seems likely they refer to an ancient agricultural practice (and, in part, magical divination) in which the leaves were used to test the heat of hay-ricks. Both species were common in traditional hay-meadows, and would be cut in full leaf. Once stacked the leaves gradually became more brittle as they dried, and their pliability was a useful indicator of the amount of moisture they contained and hence of the general state of the rick. Farmers would pull a fire-leaf from the heart of the rick, give it a twist and decide whether their hay was in danger of becoming an over-dried fire risk.

The blade-like leaves also had the kind of bold, sweeping profile that attracted Mary Anne Clifford, and the paintings are almost certainly by her.

Ribwort plantain
Plantago lanceolata
June 1850
Waysides, grassland

Hoary plantain
Plantago media
Waysides and older grassland on more chalky soils. Still occurs on the lawn at Frampton Court

Syngenesia Polygamia Superflua
Tussilago Farfara Common Coltsfoot
April 20th 1850

A cough medicine from the Frampton domestic recipe book: 'Syrup of Hyssop, Whorehound [*sic*], and Coltsfoot of each one ounce. To be put in a half-pint Bottle, and filled up with cold-drawn Linseed oil. Take a tablespoon when the cough is troublesome.'

Coltsfoot

Tussilago farfara
April 20th 1850
Disturbed, waste and open ground
Local name: hoofs (from the shape of
the leaves)

Bellis Perennis Common Daisy Frampton March 16th 1840

Syngenesia Polygamia Superflua

Local names for the ox-eye daisy: moons, moon daisy, and mathen in Tortworth, a village ten miles south of Frampton, which is famous for its thousand-year-old chestnut tree.

Syngenesia Polygamia Superflua
Chrysanthemum Leucanthemum
Oxeye Daisy June 6th 1846 Frampton

Sonchus Oleraceus Common Sow-thistle
Syngenesia Polygamia Equalis
November 6th 1844

Syngenesia Polygamia Superflua
Senecio Vulgaris Common Groundsel
Sept 8th 1843 Frampton

1	2	3	4
Ox-eye daisy	**Smooth sow-thistle**	**Daisy**	**Groundsel**
Leucanthemum vulgare	*Sonchus oleraceus*	*Bellis perennis*	*Senecio vulgaris*
June 6th 1846, Frampton	November 6th 1844	March 16th 1840, Frampton	September 8th 1843
Waysides, meadows	Waste and cultivated ground	Grassy places	Waste and cultivated ground

The Vicarage Lane

Byways

The Severn Vale, low-lying and marshy, was once reckoned to have some of the worst roads in Gloucestershire. But Frampton itself was fortunate in lying over large deposits of gravel, and according to T. Rudge, the author of *A General View of the Agriculture of the County of Gloucester* (1807), this was dug out and strewn on the local roads to help create level, well-drained surfaces. The village also had the advantage of a turnpike road linking it with the main Bristol to Gloucester road, and a network of recognized public footpaths, laid out during the enclosure of 1815. The Clifford women would have had little difficulty moving about in the neighbourhood of the village, but expeditions further afield would have involved carriages and altogether more hazardous journeys. In the early part of the nineteenth century the majority of roads were made up and repaired with whatever stone was nearest to hand, and in the Cotswolds, for instance, this meant a friable limestone which was weakened by frost and pulverized by even quite light traffic. Certainly the lanes leading to Stancombe Park would have been narrow, bumpy, deep in chalky mud for much of the year, and without the stable verges we associate with such country lanes today. For the best wayside flowers the Cliffords could well have looked to the green lanes that link the Frampton farms with the grazing marshes by the Severn. These still have the immensely wide grassy verges that were intended to give the commuting animals some extra forage, and a fine mixture of meadow flowers and field weeds.

A large number of common names have been recorded in Gloucestershire, including bedwine, bethwind, honesty, half-wood, withwind, willow-wind, most of which are shared with many other counties. Tuzzy-muzzy appears to be peculiar to Gloucestershire, and is probably a reference to the way the creamy-white flowers, and later the feathery seed plumes, are bunched among the leaves like small posies (often called tuzzy-muzzies until the last century).

But old man's beard is one of the quintessential plants of country lanes, and the name which John Gerard himself coined in the late sixteenth century is still the best. It 'is called commonly *Viorna quasi vias ornans*, of decking and adorning waies and hedges, where people travell, and thereupon I have named it the Traveilers Ioie.'

Traveller's joy or Old man's beard
Clematis vitalba
Hedges and scrub, especially on
lime-rich soils

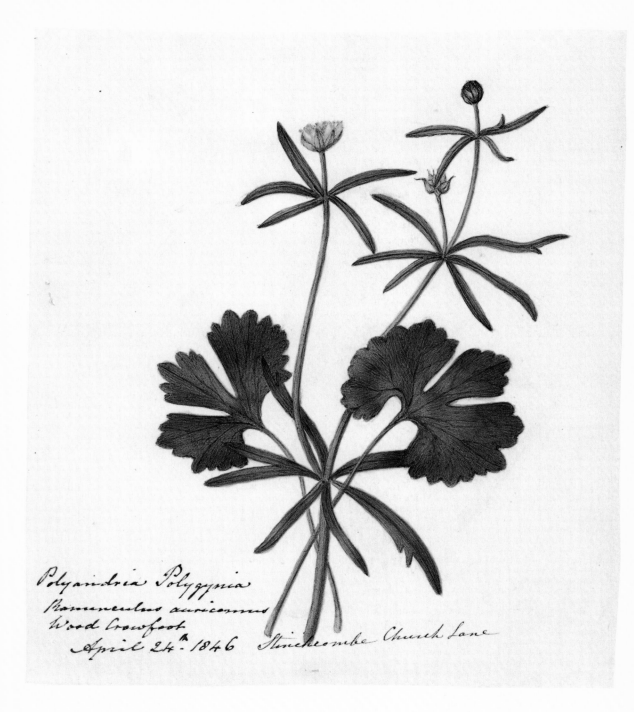

Polyandria Polygynia
Ranunculus auricomus
Wood Crowfoot
April 24th 1846   Stinchcombe Church Lane

Goldilocks buttercup
Ranunculus auricomus
April 24th 1846, Stinchcombe
Church Lane
(Still at this site, 1984)
Frequent in woods, on shady banks
and old-established grassland

Hexandria Monogynia

Berberis Vulgaris Common Barberry May 1847

Never common, even as a planted hedgerow shrub, and very scarce since it was discovered to be a host to the black rust fungus that can infest wheat crops and was therefore subject to systematic removal.

Barberry
Berberis vulgaris
May 1847
Occasional in hedgerows

Stellaria Holostea Greater Stitchwort
Decandria Trigynia
Stancombe June 11ᵗʰ – 1838

Greater stitchwort
Stellaria holostea
June 11th 1838, Stancombe
Hedge-banks, waysides, woods
Local name: wedding flowers

Stancombe June 6ᵗʰ 1838
Lychnis dioica Campion
Decandria Pentagynia

Decandria Trigynia
Silene inflata Bladder Catchfly
June 1847

Bladder campion
Silene vulgaris
June 1847
Waysides and light grassland

Red campion
Silene dioica
June 6th 1838, Stancombe
Hedge-banks, waysides, woods
Local names: butchers, butcher's cow,
bachelor's buttons, Billy button

Monadelphia Decandria
Geranium nodosum
Knotty Crane's bill
C C August 21st 1846

Knotted cranesbill
Geranium nodosum
August 21st 1846, Charlotte Clifford
An occasional garden escape

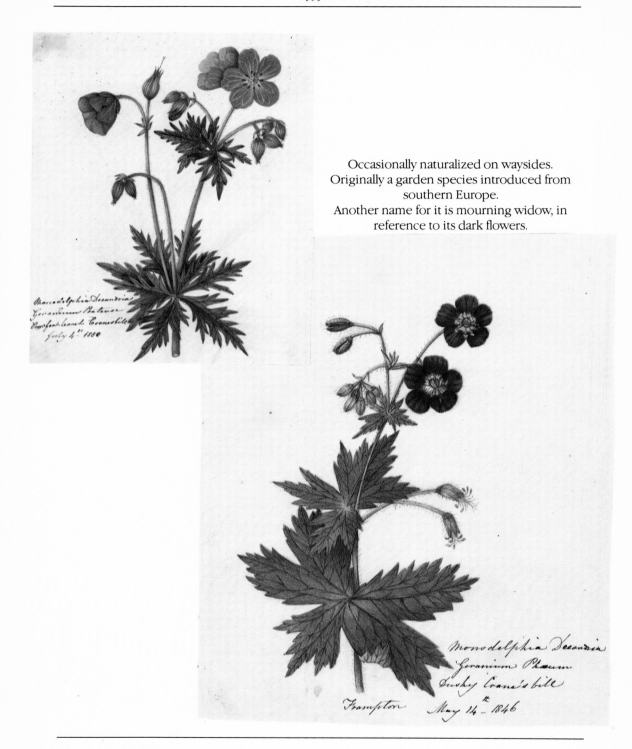

Occasionally naturalized on waysides.
Originally a garden species introduced from
southern Europe.
Another name for it is mourning widow, in
reference to its dark flowers.

Meadow cranesbill
Geranium pratense
July 4th 1850
Waysides and grassland on lime-rich
soils

Dusky cranesbill
Geranium phaeum
May 14th 1846, Frampton

Monadelphia Decandria

Geranium dissectum Jagged leaved Crane's-bill

Leamington August 1845

Wild geraniums are a feature of chalky grasslands, and meadow cranesbill in particular can colour whole stretches of Cotswold waysides in June and July. Two of the other species were originally garden introductions that have become naturalized here and there, and it is impossible to say whether they were painted from naturalized or garden specimens. If the dusky cranesbill was 'wild' it is a find which anticipates the first county record (by Miss Millard of Gloucester in 1847) by a year.

Incidentally, the treatment of rather similarly structured flowers from within a single family emphasizes the contrasting styles of at least two of the Cliffords. Charlotte's knotted cranesbill has a liveliness - a knottiness, one is tempted to say - that the other artists here could not quite achieve.

Cut-leaved cranesbill
Geranium dissectum
August 1845, ?Leamington
Waste ground and waysides

A ditch at Oldbury-on-Severn, a village about ten miles south of Frampton, is one of the very few places in Britain where a white-flowered variety of this species has been found.

Agrimony
Agrimonia eupatoria
September 4th 1849
Waysides, grasslands

Wild strawberry
Fragaria vesca
Banks, waysides, open woods

Of the handful of species that the Cliffords identified wrongly, this willow-herb is by far the most interesting and the most excusable. It is labelled as 'Great hairy willowherb or Codlings and Cream' (one of the very few vernacular names quoted by them) but it is plain from the lack of stem hairs, the flower-bud shape and the long, snake's-tongue stamens that the species is in fact rosebay willow-herb. This is now a common and conspicuous adornment of railway banks, car parks and the like, and has vastly increased even in its natural habitat in woodland clearings. In the 1960s Sir Edward Salisbury was able to write that 'I have seen a Gloucestershire woodland in early September as though in a summer snowstorm with the multitudes of plumed seeds that appeared in the air.' Back in the mid-nineteenth century the distinguished botanist Edwin Lees thought 'that it would be fanciful to consider it indigenous' in the Cotswolds.

Ironically, it was the devastation caused by two World Wars that gave rosebay the boost from which it has never looked back. It has a liking for open ground that has recently been burned over (it is known as fireweed in America) and the clear felling of so much woodland in the First War and the bombing of cities during the Second provided perfect conditions for its expansion.

It's possible that this was the first specimen the Cliffords had seen, and it is forgivable if they took it for a curious variety of the great willow-herb. And there is a suggestion at the foot of the painting that they were not entirely sure of the identification, for what looks like an alternative name is tantalizingly cut off at the top of the word 'or'.

Rosebay willow-herb
Epilobium angustifolium
Greatly increased in waysides and
waste ground

Didynamia Angiospermia

Antirrhinum Cymbalaria June 16ᵗʰ 1847

Ivy-leaved Toadflax

William Baxter, curator of the Oxford Botanic Garden, whose book on British flowering plants was used by the Cliffords, described 'this very pretty plant' as 'a native of Italy,...said to have been originally introduced into England by means of its seeds having been brought in some marble sculptures from that country to Oxford, where it has long established itself on the walls of the Colleges, gardens, &c. in such abundance as to have obtained the name of "Oxford-weed"'. This little snapdragon, introduced as a garden plant from southern Europe in 1617, is virtually unknown from natural habitats in this country. Yet it flourishes on old walls, and the rather splayed-out arrangement of the illustrated plant disguises the mechanism which has made it so successful in man-made surroundings. When it is in bloom the stalks bend *towards* the light; once the flowers have been succeeded by the oval seed-heads they bend *away* from the light, so that the seeds are more likely to be shed into cracks and joints in the supporting wall.

Ivy-leaved toadflax
Cymbalaria muralis
June 16th 1847
Walls, pavements (currently in great
quantities on the walls and steps of
Frampton Court itself)
Local name: mother-of-thousands

Solanum Dulcamara Woody Nightshade
Pentandria Monogynia   *July 1840*

Didynamia Angiospermia

Antirrhinum Linaria
Common Toad Flax

Woody nightshade or Bittersweet
Solanum dulcamara
July 1840
Waysides, damp places
Local name: dwale (more commonly found as a
colloquial name for deadly nightshade, *Atropa
belladonna.*)

Common toadflax
Linaria vulgaris
Waysides, waste ground
Local names: butter and eggs, eggs and
bacon

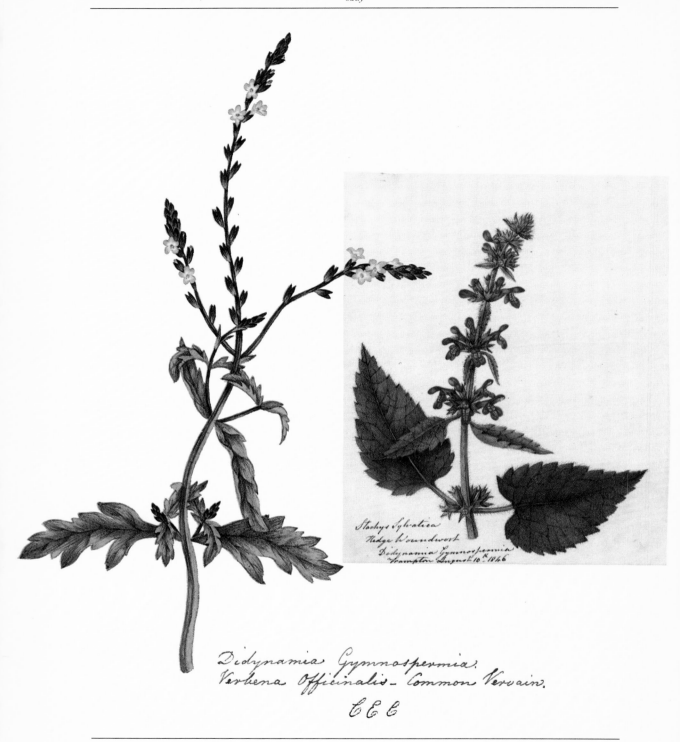

Didynamia Gymnospermia.
Verbena Officinalis – Common Vervain.
C. E. C.

Vervain
Verbena officinalis
Catherine Elizabeth Clifford
Locally common on waysides and in
grassy places
Accredited to Catherine Elizabeth
Clifford, though in a different hand to
the caption

Hedge woundwort
Stachys sylvatica
August 10th 1846, Frampton
Waysides, woods

Didynamia Gymnospermia
Nepeta Cataria Common Catmint
Frampton Sept. 30. 1850

Although this is unquestionably our native catmint, it is hard to be certain that it was painted from a wild specimen. Catmint has always been a rather scarce and local flower, and was not officially recorded for the Frampton area until the end of the nineteenth century. On the other hand it was widely planted in herb gardens. The catmint which has now almost completely replaced it in cultivation, the blue-grey-leaved *Nepeta* x *faassenii*, was introduced from the Caucasus about 1800, but was initially regarded as being far too drab to encourage in gardens. It was nearly a hundred years before Gertrude Jekyll changed its fortunes by championing it as a soft, border-edging plant 'that can hardly be overpraised'.

Catmint
Nepeta cataria
September 30th 1850, Frampton
Waysides and waste places; scarce

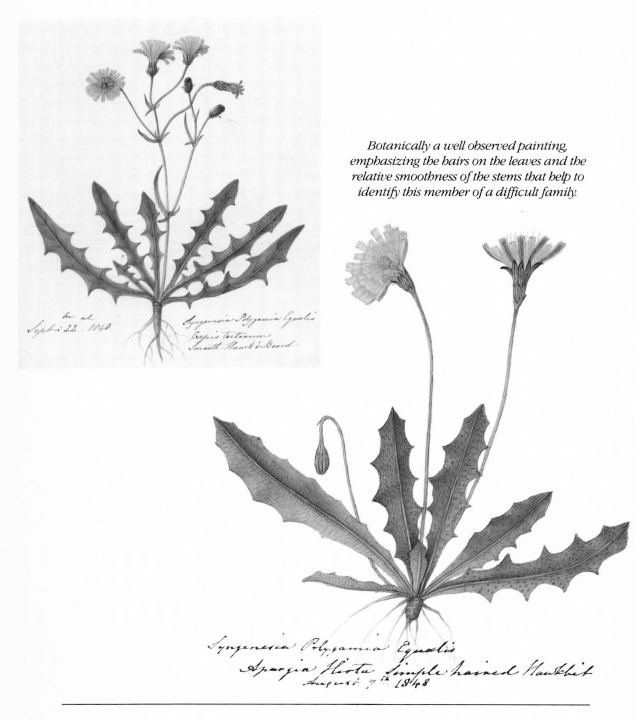

Botanically a well observed painting, emphasizing the hairs on the leaves and the relative smoothness of the stems that help to identify this member of a difficult family.

Smooth hawksbeard

Crepis capillaris
September 22nd 1848
Waysides, rough grassland

Lesser hawkbit

Leontodon taraxacoides
August 7th 1848
Waysides, grassy places

2

Syngenesia Polygamia Superflua
Senecio Jacobaea Common Ragwort
August 15th 1848

3

1

Syngenesia Polygamia Equalis
Carduus acanthoides Welted Thistle

C E C

Syngenesia Polygamia Frustranea
Centaurea Nigra
Black Soft Knapweed

*Attributed to Catherine Elizabeth in a
different hand from the original caption.*

1	2	3
Spear thistle	**Common ragwort**	**Common knapweed**
Cirsium vulgare	*Senecio jacobaea*	*Centaurea nigra*
Waysides, rough grassland	August 15th 1848	Catherine Elizabeth Clifford
Incorrectly labelled as the somewhat	Waysides, rough grassland	Waysides, grassy places
similar welted thistle, *Carduus*	Local name: summer farewell	Local names: black soap, hardheads,
acanthoides		loggerheads, clobweed

The Cotswold Hedge

The following six shrubs (and two woody climbers) make up the backbone of most of the hedges in the Cotswolds and the Vale of Berkeley, just as they would have done in the early nineteenth century. This is not to say that the hedges *look* the same today. Although the area has been less troubled by hedgerow clearance than the neighbouring Midlands, few of the hedges are any longer maintained by hand. Most are cut annually by mechanical flails which reduce the growing shoots to a fine mulch. Traditionally the outward and upward growth was cut back much less frequently - maybe only once every five to ten years - and was put to good use. Hazel, for instance, was used in making sheep hurdles. Good quality maple went for the furniture trade. The hard, white wood of dogwood was excellent for skewers (hence the local name skiver-tree). and most of the rougher trimmings were bundled up for firewood. The 1815 Enclosure Award for Frampton has a revealing aside about the contemporary value of hedges. It specifies that the original 'owners' of hedges may not cut them after the re-allotment of lands ordered by the Award, but that they must be left for the 'profit and benefit' of the new holders.

The enclosure of Frampton in 1815 no doubt increased the number of hedges in the area. The old open fields were divided up with new, straight (and still surviving) rows of blackthorn, elm and hawthorn, and in once instance with an unusual mix of hawthorn and privet, with a privet inserted roughly every fifth bush. Privet had been popular as a garden hedging plant since the late sixteenth century, but it is extremely unusual to see it deliberately used in farm hedges.

The massive increase in the proportion of hawthorn is probably the one significant botanical difference between pre- and post-1815 hedges in the area, and may help to explain why the particular hawthorn represented here is something of a puzzler. Although it is labelled with one of the more unusual contemporary names (medlar hawthorn - *Mespilus oxyacanthoides*) of our common hawthorn, *Crataegus monogyna*, the plant in the illustration has some characteristics of the much scarcer Midland and woodland hawthorn (now *C. laevigata*). The leaves are blunter and less deeply cut, and the flowers larger than one would expect to see in a common hawthorn. (Other differences uncheckable from the painting are the laxer habit of the woodland hawthorn, and the fact that it has two, rather than one seed in its berries.) The most likely possibility is that it is a hybrid between the two species; these can still be found in old hedges around Stancombe.

If so, it may be one of the Cliffords' most interesting finds. Woodland hawthorn and its hybrids are on the extreme south-western edge of their range in Gloucestershire, and were no doubt confined, as now, to ancient hedges and woods on the clay. Although woodland hawthorn was recognized as a separate species by 1790 in France, British botanical textbooks were still regarding hawthorns with blunt leaves and two-seeded berries as mere varieties of the common one until the middle of the nineteenth century. The first unequivocal record from the Frampton area is in 1869, twenty years after this painting was made.

Pentandria Monogynia
Hedera Helix Common Ivy

Ivy
Hedera helix

Acer Campestre Common Maple
Octandria Monogynia
Stancombe June 12th – 1845

Field maple
Acer campestre
June 12th 1845, Stancombe
Local name: maplin tree

Monoecia Polyandria
Corylus Avellana Common Hazel
April & June 1847

It is probably just a coincidence that the artist picked a hybrid to illustrate her hawthorn, but there is a possibility that the planting of miles of quickthorn hedges in a landscape which already contained woodland hawthorn had greatly increased the frequency of the hybrid. The hybrid may even have increased at the expense of the woodland species, and one botanical historian, David Elliston Allen, has a theory that the latter may once have been common enough to be the original May. It generally comes into flower a week or two before the common hawthorn, whose late blooming (sometimes in June in our current run of late summers) always made its claim to be the flower of the month rather curious. Adding the eleven days by which the calendar was shifted forward during the revision of 1752, the woodland hawthorn was fairly certain to have been in flower on Old May Day.

Hazel
Corylus avellana
April and June 1847 (to include the
young nuts)

Sixandria Monogynia
Prunus Spinosa Sloe Cherry
April & June 1847

Lonicera Periclymenum Communis Honeysuckle
Pentandria Monogynia H. P.— July 17th 1846

Diandria Monogynia

Ligustrum Vulgare
Common Privet
July 18th 1850

Cornus Sanguinea Wild Cornel
Tetrandria Monogynia

1	2	3	4
Blackthorn	**Wild privet**	**Honeysuckle**	**Dogwood**
Prunus spinosa	*Ligustrum vulgare*	*Lonicera periclymenum*	*Swida sanguinea*
April and June 1847 (to include the leaves, which emerge after the flowers) Local names: heg-pegs, egg-peg bush	July 18th 1850	July 17th 1846, (Helen Purnell?) Local names: woodbind, woodbine, woodwind	Local name: skiver-tree.

Icosandria Pentagynia
Mespilus Oxyacantha
Hawthorn Medlar
May 24th 1849

One other fact is suggestive of woodland hawthorn being the original May-flower. There is an ancient superstition that May blossom must never be brought into a house for fear that a death will occur there. It is hard to see any feature of common hawthorn which could account for this belief, but the blossoms of the woodland hawthorn smell strongly and sinisterly of rotten meat, which could explain its reputation as a harbinger of death. As woodland hawthorn declined with the clearance of old woods and hedges and its common relative spread, it is easy to see how the superstition could have been transferred to the more familiar species.

Hawthorn
Crataegus species
May 24th 1849
Local names: haw-tree, heg-peg bush
(see blackthorn opposite), May fruit

Job. Browning - Tony Draper.

Woodlands

According to the Domesday Book in 1086, the manor of Frampton contained a huge wood 'one mile long, and three furlongs broad'. There was little chance of this surviving, given the quality of the soil underneath, and by the early part of the nineteenth century it had all been cleared for agriculture. The only woodlands shown on estate maps of the time all appear to be plantation, probably established during the previous hundred years. The flowers of these essentially artificial woods would not have been much different from those growing along nearby hedge-banks. But long established woodland, where primroses and anemones and archangel grew, had survived on the Cotswold scarp, and it is here that the Cliffords painted a remarkable collection of the special flowers of ancient woodland. They are wholly characteristic of the Cotswolds, and, taken together, could not have been assembled anywhere else in the country. There are the typical species of limestone woods, lily-of-the-valley, wintergreen, nettle-leaved bellflower; the beechwood orchids and mezereon; and local specialities and rarities like green hellebore.

The Cliffords were fortunate in having access to Stancombe Park, which had its own expanses of private woodland. Many of the species are labelled as being painted there. But the women were plainly not deterred either by the taint of danger that still clung to forest areas, or by the difficulty of the terrain. To judge by the annotations in her books, Marianne Phelps and (C.M. Clifford?) frequently visited the steep woods aound Alderley and Wotton-under-Edge, a few miles to the south of Stancombe.

Polyandria Polygynia
Helleborus viridis Green Hellebore

Yellow anemone is an occasional garden
escape, and there was a naturalized colony
near Haresfield vicarage (three miles to the
east of Frampton) in the nineteenth century.

Anemone nemorosa 1   Wood Anemone
Anemone Ranunculoides 2 Yellow Wood Anemone
Polyandria Polygynia

Wood anemone and Yellow anemone
Anemone nemorosa and Anemone ranunculoides
Wood anemone is common in old woods and
on shady hedge-banks.
Local names: ladies' nightcap, nemony,
wind-flower

Green hellebore
Helleborus viridis
Accredited to Catherine Elizabeth Clifford in a
different hand from the caption.
Scarce in woods and shady places on chalkier
soils. Sometimes a relic of old gardens

Aquilegia Vulgaris Common Columbine
Polyandria Pentagynia

Columbine
Aquilegia vulgaris
Occasional in woods and pasture on
the limestone.
Local name: granny's nightcap

Viola Odorata April 6 -1840

Pentandria Monogynia

J.L. Knapp's *Journal of a Naturalist* describes 'One application of flowers at this season I have noticed, which, though perhaps it is local, yet it has a remarkably pretty effect, forming for the time one of the gayest little shrubs that can be seen. A small branch or long spray of the white-thorn, with all its spines uninjured, is selected; and on these its alternate thorns, a white and a blue violet, plucked from their stalks, are stuck upright in succession, until the thorns are covered, and when placed in a flower-pot of moss, has perfectly the appearance of a beautiful vernal flowering dwarf shrub, and as long as it remains fresh is an object of surprise and delight.'

(This painting was not drawn from life but was partly modelled on the illustration in Smith and Sowerby's English Botany*, volume XI plate 762 (1800). This probably explains the late summer date)*

Decandria Pentagynia
Oxalis Acetosella Common Wood Sorrel
August 1846

Sweet violet
Viola odorata
April 6th 1840 (Compare Charlotte
Anne Purnell's and Charlotte Clifford's
pictures of the same plant, page 7)
Quite common, woods and
hedge-banks

Wood sorrel
Oxalis acetosella
August 1846
Quite common in old woods and on
shady hedge-banks.
Local names: cuckoo's victuals,
cuckoo's bread and cheese, cuckoo's
meat, green sauce

Wood sorrel, as its 'cuckoo' names testify, is a familiar woodland flower of springtime, and in an entry in her diary for December 11th 1860, Charlotte Clifford (not, I think, responsible for this painting) copied out a passage on the appropriateness of wood sorrel as a Whitsun flower. It was from *The Garland of the Year* for June 1852. This was a popular botanical publication at the time, and the passage is a striking example of the fashion for using the lives of plants as moral parables.

'No less an authority than...Gerarde himself thus writes of the wood sorrel - "Apothecaries and herbalists call it alleluya and cuckowe's meat...either because the cuckowe feedeth thereon, or by reason that when it springeth forth the cuckowe singeth most, at which time alleluya was wont to be sung in our Churches."

'A more beautiful floral emblem of praise could not be selected than this exquisitely sensitive little plant. Coming forth at the first summons of spring it continues to adorn the woods with its bright triple leaves, until the fading foliage of autumn consigns it to a living grave. Even then, the flower-searcher may discover here and there a delicately-folded leaf looking out from the desolation and death by which it is surrounded. For the alleluya, fragile though it be, can brave the roughest gales, and weather the wildest storms, bowing its meek head beneath the clouds, and looking up with joy, to greet the sunshine. Sweet and precious are the lessons which this little woodland plant may teach us - lessons of humble faith, and constant loving praise. Teaching us that, as the shrinking wood sorrel finds protection in its triple leaves, so our souls, strengthened by the three-fold gifts of the Holy Ghost, should bow in meek submission to the trials of their mortal existence. Ever praising, never repining bearing all sorrow; thankful for all joys! And, like the little sylvan emblem of praise, still singing in sunshine and in storm, in prosperity and adversity, their grateful alleluyas.'

A nicely laid-out picture which emphasizes the leathery flatness of the leaves. They were once dried and used as bookmarks, hence the alternative name of Bible leaf.

Tutsan

Hypericum androsaemum
August 1849
Rare in old woods and lanes, but rather
more frequent in the hilly, wooded
country around Stinchcombe.
Recorded from woods near Alderley by
Marianne Phelps

Orpine, or livelong, is a member of one of our few truly succulent plant families. Its leaves dry and shrink very slowly, and in neighbouring Wiltshire John Aubrey recorded how this characteristic was used in an ancient midsummer divination ritual: 'I remember, the mayds (especially the Cooke mayds and Dayrymades) would stick-up in some chinkes of the joists, etc., Midsommer-men, which are slips of Orpin. They placed them by paires, sc: one for such a man, the other for such a mayd his sweetheart, and accordingly as the Orpin did incline to, or recline from the other, that there would be love or aversion; if either did wither, death.' (From *Remains of Gentilisme and Judaisme*, 1686-7)

Orpine
Sedum telephium
August 3rd 1850
Scarce at woodland edges and on old
hedge-banks. Occasionally colonizes
drystone walls

2

1

Geum Urbanum
Common Avens   *Icosandria Polygynia*

3

Icosandria Polygynia
Geum Rivale Water   Avens
April 1848

Chrysosplenium Alternifolium
Alternate leaved Golden Saxifrage
Decandria Digynia
Stancombe

1	2	3
Water avens	**Wood avens or Herb Bennet**	**Alternate-leaved golden saxifrage**
Geum rivale	*Geum urbanum*	*Chrysosplenium alternifolium*
April 1848	Woods and waysides	Stancombe
Woods, riversides and damp banks		Scarce by shady stream-sides

Diandria Monogynia   Frampton August 28th 1837
Circea Lutetiana Enchanter's nightshade

Decandria Monogynia
Pyrola minor — Lesser Wintergreen:

Enchanter's nightshade
Circaea lutetiana
August 28th 1837
Woods, shady waste places

Lesser wintergreen
Pyrola minor
Date illegible
Rare, and almost confined in
Gloucestershire to woods on the
limestone

Dioecia Enneandria
Perenial Mercury Mercurialis Perennis May 1847
From Stancombe —

Daphne Mezereon. Spurge Olive CEC
Octandria Monogynia

This shrub, well known from gardens for its fragrant, February blooms, has always been local and rare. It was not recorded from the wild in Britain until 1752, and though it has persisted in the Cotswolds, there has never been an official record from any of the Cliffords' favourite haunts (though Marianne Phelps records seeing it in Kilcote Woods, near Wotton-under-Edge).

It has been called paradise plant in Gloucestershire, and there's little doubt that many of the specimens in cottage gardens came originally from the wild. Now - perhaps in consequence - it is so rare that even picking a spray is forbidden by law. This makes the white gash where the twig has been pulled from the stem a rather poignant feature of this painting to our modern eyes. It may be a purely visual effect, to balance the side-shoot on the right, or a gothic finish for a woody stem that couldn't simply end in the same fashion as a green stem. But for us it also makes a statement about the period in which the painting was made, and its unawareness of the fragility of our wild plants.

Mezereon	**Dog's mercury**
Daphne mezereum	*Mercurialis perennis*
CEC (for Catherine Elizabeth Clifford)	May 1847, 'From Frampton'
added in pencil	Woods, old hedge-banks
Rare in woods on lime-rich soils	

Pentandria Monogynia

Campanula Trachelium   *Nettlebeaved Companule*

Nettle-leaved bellflower
Campanula trachelium
Quite common in woods on lime-rich
soils

Local name: town clock, from the arrangement of the flowers at the end of the stalk, opposed to each other like the faces of a town-hall clock. Recorded from woods near Alderley by Marianne Phelps.

Employs a technique of emphasizing the whiteness of the flowers that none of the other women used. Recorded from a number of Cotswold woods by Marianne Phelps.

Moschatel
Adoxa moschatellina
April 20th 1840
Woods, shady banks

Woodruff
Galium odoratum
June 1850, (Helen Purnell?)
Old woods, shady banks

Galeobdolon Luteum Yellow Weaselsnout Yellow Archangel. *Didynamia Gymnospermia*

Didynamia Gymnospermia.
Teucrium Scorodonia.—Wood Germander.

CEC

Yellow archangel
Lamiastrum galeobdolon
Old woods and shady banks
Local name: weasel-snout, a reference
to the shape of the flowers (and also,
perhaps, to the rather strong smell of
the leaves)

Wood sage
Teucrium scorodonia
CEC (for Catherine Elizabeth Clifford) added
in a different hand from the caption
Frequent in old woods and heaths
In the Dursley area wood sage was used to
make a spring drink against rheumatism

Didynamia Gymnospermia.
Ajuga reptans — Common Bugle —

Bugle

Ajuga reptans
Woods, banks, meadows Local name:
thunder-and-lightning, perhaps a
reference to the colours of the leaves,
glistening grey-blue shot through with
copper

Frampton April 20th 1839

Primula Vulgaris
Common Primrose
Pentandria Monogynia

Primrose
Primula vulgaris
April 20th 1839, Frampton
Frequent but rather local in woodland
rides and clearings, churchyards, etc

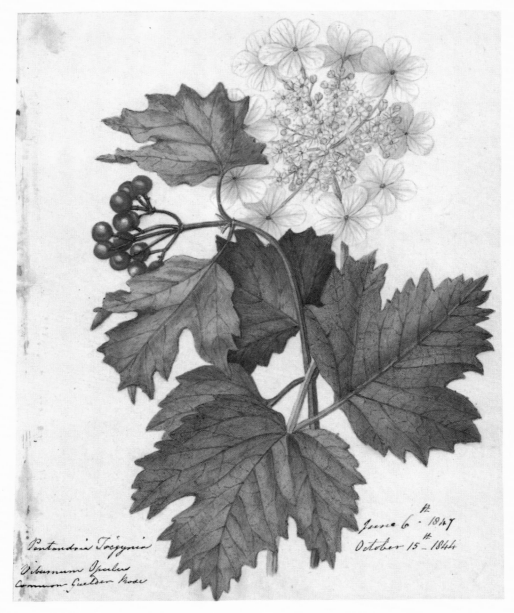

Pentandria Trigynia
Viburnum Opulus
Common Guelder Rose

June 6th 1847
October 15th 1844

*The three following splendidly uninhibited paintings by Mary Anne Clifford show
considerable confidence in their arrangement on the page, not least in the guelder rose,
where the flowers were added three years after the remainder of the painting. And the
concentration on the large lower leaves of the common valerian, which have been raised up
close to the blossom, emphasizes the lushness of this species, which is so typical of luxuriant
woodland edges in high summer.*

Guelder rose

Viburnum opulus
June 6th 1847 (flowers); October 15th
1844 (berries)
Fairly frequent, woods and
stream-sides
Local name: king's crown

Monoecia Polyandria

Arum Maculatum

Common Cuckowpint or Wake Robin

Lords and ladies or Cuckoo pint
Arum maculatum
Woods, hedge-banks
Local names: wakerobin, cows and
calves, snake's victuals

Triandria Monogynia
Valeriana Officinalis
'Great Wild Valerian
Nibley Lane 1849

Common valerian
Valeriana officinalis
1849, Nibley Lane.
Frequent, woodland edges, ditches,
damp grassland

Convalaria Majalis
Lilly of the Valley Solomon's seal

Hexandria Monogynia
Stancombe May 1845

February 1839 Frampton *Galanthus, Snowdrop*

Hexandria Monogynia

Snowdrop
Galanthus nivalis
February 1839, Frampton
Naturalized from gardens in woods,
waysides, churchyards, etc.
Local name: Candlemas bells

Lily-of-the-valley
Convallaria majalis
May 1845, Stancombe
Rather scarce in woods on the limestone
Recorded from Kilcote and Westidge
Woods, near Wotton-under-Edge, by
Marianne Phelps

So much have these three attractive members of the lily family moved back and forth between gardens and the wild that it is often hard to tell the origins of particular colonies. Lily-of-the-valley, for instance, though occasionally naturalized near gardens, is an undisputed native of the Cotswold woods. Snowdrop, though often growing in huge quantities, is invariably a garden escape.

Bluebells, of course, are a widespread native, but they too are often transplanted into gardens, only to escape again. *White* bluebells are such a conspicuous feature of some hedge-banks around the Frampton area, frequently growing in the absence of any blue-flowered specimens, that there is a possibility that they were a parish favourite - brought out of the woods, and repeatedly passed around and swapped by village gardeners.

Bluebell
Endymion non-scriptus
Mrs. H. Clifford (presumably Marianne
Phelps, after her marriage to Henry
Clifford)
Woods, shady banks

Orchids

The orchid paintings are among the most accomplished and botanically interesting of the whole collection. They make an impressively comprehensive group too. Twelve different species are portrayed, and no other plant family was so thoroughly and successfully sought out by the Cliffords. Since most of the species were probably no more common or widespread then than now, it looks as if they had a special fascination with this glamorous family, and were willing to venture into some fairly rough and thorny country after them. The majority of the specimens were found on the hills at Stinchcombe, but unnibbled flowering spikes would have been few and far between on the heavily grazed downland, and the women would have had more luck in the rougher grass and scrub where the downs merged with the woods, and, for white helleborine and yellow bird's-nest, in the shade of the beechwoods themselves.

Recorded by 'CMC' (probably Marianne's daughter, Constance M. Clifford) 'about the Gloucester & Berkeley canal between Fretherne and Whitminster Bridge. Also an albino specimen'. (Still occurs on gravelly soils in Frampton, as well as on the hills round Stinchcombe.)

Bee orchid
Ophrys apifera
Stancombe
Dry grassland. Local and erratic in
appearance

Gynandria Monandria

1 Orchis bifolia Butterfly Orchis
2 Listera ovata Common Twayblade
C. A. P. Stancombe Park

3 Epipactis grandiflora
Large White Helleborine
R. C. Stancombe June 24 - 1839

An intriguing composite painting, done from specimens in Stancombe Park in June 1839. Charlotte Anne Purnell painted the butterfly orchid and the twayblade, and Rosamond Clifford interwove the white helleborine as if it lay underneath the other specimens. All three species are to scale, virtually life-size.

1	2	3
Greater butterfly orchid	**Common twayblade**	**White helleborine**
Platanthera chlorantha	*Listera ovata*	*Cephalanthera damasonium*
June 24th 1839, Charlotte Anne Purnell	Charlotte Anne Purnell	Rosamond Clifford
Locally frequent in woodland clearings and edges and scrub, chiefly on lime-rich soils. (Greater and lesser butterfly orchids were not recognized as separate species at this time)	Woods, scrub, especially on limy soils	Locally frequent in beechwoods

Gynandria Monandria:
Ophrys Muscifera – Fly Ophrys –
June 19th 1843.

Fly orchid

Ophrys insectifera
June 19th 1843, Charlotte Anne Purnell
Scrub, light woodland, on limy soils.
Locally frequent

Gynandria Monandria
Orchis Mascula
Early Purple Orchis   Stancombe   June 1839

Early purple orchid
Orchis mascula
June 1839, Stancombe
Woods, grassland and scrub.
Local names: bloody fingers,
bloody man's fingers,
dead man's fingers, dead man's hand,
goosey-ganders

Two species which have declined over the last two decades, largely because of habitat loss. The burnt orchid, which prefers short, dry downland turf, is on the northern edge of its range in Britain and never common, and there may be climatic factors involved in its decline. The green-winged, by contrast, prefers slightly damper soils and has been reduced dramatically by the ploughing and drainage of permanent pastures.

1   2

Burnt orchid and Green-winged orchid
Orchis ustulata and Orchis morio
June 1839, Stancombe, Charlotte Anne
Purnell

Secandria Monogynia
Monotropa, Yellow Bird's nest
Hypopitys

Common spotted orchid
Dactylorhiza fuchsii
June 1840, Stancombe
Grassland, especially on lime-rich soils

Yellow bird's-nest
Monotropa hypopitys
Beechwoods, rare

Gynandria Monandria
Orchis Pyramidalis
Pyramidal Orchis
Frampton July 1839

Pyramidal orchid
Anacamptis pyramidalis
July 1839, Frampton
Locally frequent, downland

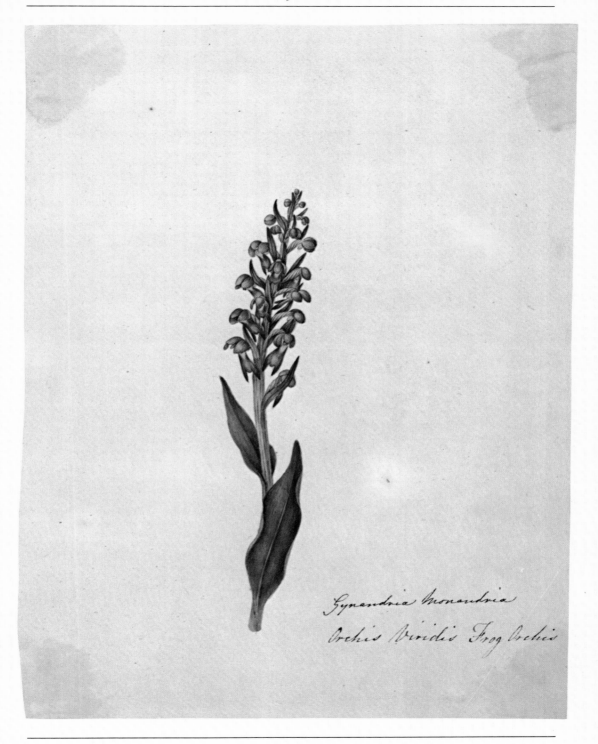

Gynandria Monandria

Orchis Viridis Frog Orchis

Frog orchid
Coeloglossum viride
Short grassland on lime-rich soils.
Rather scarce

The Parks Farm. Aug.ᵗʰ 18.ᵗʰ 1866. — *Frocester Church.*

Grasslands

Grass is the dominant crop in the Cotswolds and Severn Vale, and even over Gloucestershire as a whole accounts for half of all agricultural land. In the early nineteenth century most of this would have been permanent pasture, unploughed, unfertilized, and rich in wild flowers. Writing in 1829, J.L. Knapp wondered if the hayfields of the Vale could with any truthfulness even be called grasslands: 'A truss of our hay from these districts, brought into the London market, or exhibited as a new article of provender at a Smithfield cattle show, would occasion conversation and comment. The crop consists almost entirely of the common field scabious, loggerheads [common knapweed], and the great ox-eye daisy. There is a scattering of bent, and here and there a specimen of the better grasses; but the predominant, the staple of the crop, is scabious - it is emphatically a promiscuous herbage; yet on this rubbish do the cattle thrive, and from their milk is produced a cheese greatly esteemed for toasting.'

Today few fields are cut for hay, and those that are have mostly been reseeded with high-yield grass strains. But fragments of the kinds of grassland with which the Cliffords would have been familiar do survive. On the limestone hills near Stancombe - and especially Stinchcombe Hill - there is a fine downland turf produced by centuries of sheep grazing and very rich in dwarf flowers. At another extreme are the grazing marshes by the Severn, with their wetland plants and, occasionally, maritime species. Closest to home for the Cliffords was Rosamond's Green, a rougher piece of grassland altogether, but no doubt sporting cowslips and cuckoo-flowers in spring, just as it does today.

Polyandria Monogynia:
Cistus Helianthemum— Dwarf Cistus—
or Vulgare.
C.A.P.

Polyadelphia Polyandria
Hypericum montanum
August 1847 Stancombe

Common rock-rose
Helianthemum chamaecistus
Charlotte Anne Purnell
Limestone grassland

Pale St. John's wort
Hypericum montanum
(Specific name added to caption in
pencil)
Scarce and local on lime-rich grassland
in Cotswolds

Diadelphia Octandria.
Polygala Vulgaris. Common Milkwort.
June 25th 1843.

Polyadelphia Polgandria
Hypericum perforatum Perforated St. John's Wort
Leamington Sept.r 1845

Common milkwort

Polygala vulgaris
June 25th 1843
Short grassland, especially on chalkier
soils

Perforate St. John's wort

Hypericum perforatum
September 1845, Leamington
Rough pastures, waysides, woodland
clearings

1   2

Yellow vetchling and Tufted vetch
Lathyrus aphaca and Vicia cracca
June 1846, Stinchcombe Road
Both common in rough grassland,
woodland clearings and waysides

Horseshoe vetch
Hippocrepis comosa
July 4th 1843 (caption in Charlotte
Anne Purnell's hand)
Limestone grassland

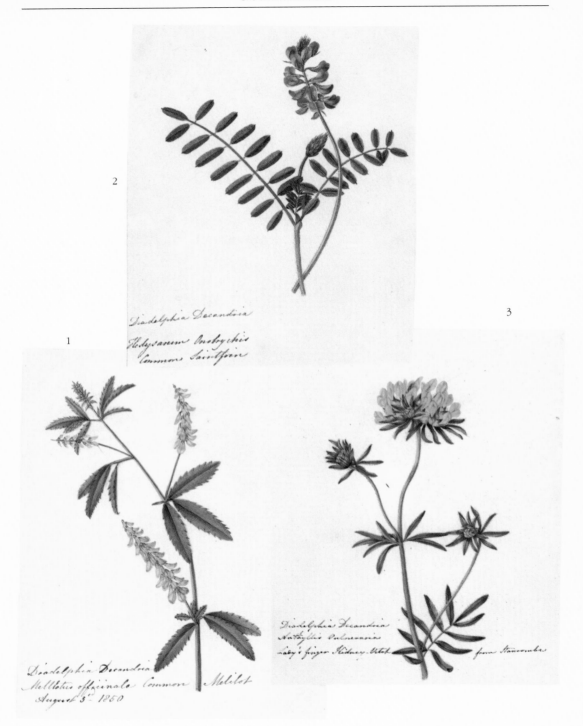

1	2	3
Ribbed melilot	**Sainfoin**	**Kidney vetch**
Melilotus officinalis	*Onobrychis viciifolia*	*Anthyllis vulneraria*
August 3rd 1850	Rough grassland and cultivated fields	Stancombe
Rough grassland, waysides, waste land	on the limestone	Limestone grassland
	Local names: thatch, zenfun.	
	Frequently cultivated as a fodder crop	
	in the Cotswolds	

Frampton
May 6th 1842

Primula veris
Pentandria Monogynia

Cowslip
Primula veris
May 6th 1842, Frampton
Pastures, waysides, downs. Still occurs
on Frampton Green

Biting stonecrop or wall-pepper is known in parts of England as welcome-home-husband-though-never-so-drunk, the longest and most cryptic of all vernacular plant names. It is hard to fathom how this dweller on downs and roof-tops acquired it - unless the expression 'a night on the tiles' is rather older than we imagine.

Biting stonecrop
Sedum acre
June 1838, Stancombe
Short grassland, drystone walls, roofs

Octandria Monogynia
Chlora Perfoliata Yellow-wort

Pentandria Monogynia
Erythrea Centaurium Common Centaury
July 21st 1847

Common centaury
Centaurium erythraea
July 21st 1847
Dry grassland, heaths, woodland rides

Yellow-wort
Blackstonia perfoliata
Limestone grassland

Pentandria Monogynia
Cynoglossum Officinale
Common Hound's Tongue

From Clevedon
M. A. C.

Gloucestershire is peculiar in having the name 'gipsy flower' for this species. Geoffrey Grigson
hints that this may be because of its tawny flowers (which the seventeenth-century
herbalist John Pechey described as a 'sordid red'). But it may have more to do with
hound's-tongue's liking for the dry commons haunted by gypsies in the Cotswolds, and with its
long association with folk medicine. It was one of the most striking examples of the doctrine of
signatures, prescribed as a protective charm against dog bites (and as a cure for them if this
failed), because of a fancied resemblance between its long, lax leaves and a hound's tongue.

Hound's-tongue
Cynoglossum officinale
'From Clevedon', Mary Anne Clifford
Dry grassland, heaths, woodland
clearings

Didynamia Angiospermia
Euphrasia officinalis Common Eyebright

Bartsia Odontites Red Bartsia
Didynamia Angiospermia

1	2	3
Yellow rattle	**Eyebright**	**Red bartsia**
Rhinanthus minor	*Euphrasia officinalis*	*Odontites verna*
June 24th 1843	Short grassland, especially on lime-rich	Grassland, waysides, cultivated fields
Pastures, meadows	soils	
Local name: cock's comb		

The common English name 'Red heath rattle' has been inserted in the caption at a later date; perhaps 'lousewort' - certainly accepted and current at the time - was a little too common for the artist's taste!

Lousewort
Pedicularis sylvatica
Damp pastures and heaths

Common broomrape
Orobanche minor
July 22nd 1843
Locally frequent on downs, meadows,
ley grassland. Parasitic on clover and
other pea-flowers

Thymus Calamintha
Calamint Thyme
August 1839

Didynamia Gymnospermia

Didynamia Gymnospermia
Clinopodium Vulgare — Wild Basil —
CEC

Wild basil

Clinopodium vulgare
CEC (for Catherine Elizabeth Clifford)
added in a different hand from the one
in the caption
Limestone grassland, waysides, open
woods

Common calamint

Calamintha ascendens
August 1839
Limestone grassland, banks,
occasionally on drystone walls. Rather
scarce and declining

Pentandria Monogynia:
Campanula Rotundifolia:- Round-leaved Campanula-
C.A.P.

Harebell
Campanula rotundifolia
Charlotte Anne Purnell
Downs, heaths, pastures

Tetrandria Monogynia
Scabiosa succisa
Devil's-bit Scabious
Sept.ᵇᵉʳ 18ᵗʰ 1850

Devil's-bit scabious
Succisa pratensis
September 18th 1850
Damp meadows and heaths. Now
scarce and declining

Tetrandria Monogynia
Scabiosa Arvensis Field Scabious

Tetrandria Monogynia
Galium verum Yellow Bedstraw
July 27ᵗʰ 1848

Field scabious
Knautia arvensis
Rough grassland, waysides
Local names: cornflower, bachelor's
buttons

Lady's bedstraw
Galium verum
July 27th 1848
Grassland, waysides

Syngenesia Polygamia Superflua
Conyza Squarrosa Plowman's Spikenard
Sept – 12 th – 1848

John Gerard gives the following explanation of the English name: 'The root is thicke, grosse, and fat, spreading about in the earth, full of strings: the fragrant smell that the root of this plant yeeldeth, may well be compared unto the savour of Cinnamon...in English it may be called the Cinamom roote, or Plowmans Spiknarde... It delighteth to grow in rough & craggie places, and in a leane soile where no moisture is: it groweth very plentifully about... divers places in the West parts of England.'

Ploughman's spikenard
Inula conyza
September 12th 1848
Limestone grassland, woodland rides
and clearings

Syngenesia Polygamia Equalis
Hieracium Pilosella Mouse-ear Hawkweed

Mouse-ear hawkweed
Hieracium pilosella
Short grassland, downs, lawns

Mountain everlasting
Antennaria dioica
A rare plant of limestone grassland and heaths in Gloucestershire but recorded occasionally from Stinchcombe Hill, which is almost certainly where the artist found it

Shaky Ground

Diadelphia Decandria *Ulex Europaeus Common Furze*
February 1846 The Park Frampton

Much of Gloucestershire lies over limestone, and acid soils are more or less confined to the extreme south of the county and to that part lying to the west of the Severn. As the Cliffords do not seem to have spent much time in these areas, it's no real surprise that the plants of acid heaths and boggy ground are the least well represented and most suspect of the collection. Only the illustration of the gorse, which can crop up on almost any poor, dry patch, is reliable, and was painted at the beginning of its flowering season inside Frampton Park. The other three species are extemely rare in Gloucestershire, and were probably all copied, although it is not impossible that they were seen by the Cliffords.

Gorse
Ulex europaeus
February 1846, Frampton Park
Locally common on heaths, woodland
borders, pastures on sandy soils

Parnassia Palustris   Pentandria Tehagynia.

Common Grass of Parnassus

1

Pentandria Monogynia

Jasione Montana Sheep's Scabious

C E C

3

Diandria Monogynia

Pinguicula Vulgaris   Common Butterwort

2

1	2	3
Grass of Parnassus	**Common butterwort**	**Sheep's-bit**
Parnassia palustris	*Pinguicula vulgaris*	*Jasione montana*
Rare in bogs and marshes, and only in east Gloucestershire.	Bogs. Very rare	Catherine Elizabeth Clifford
Copied from an illustration in Baxter's	Copied from an illustration in Smith	Heaths. Very rare
British Phaenogamous Botany	and Sowerby's *English Botany*	
(volume I plate 70 (1834))	(volume I plate 70 (1790))	

Wetlands

Perhaps the feature of the early nineteenth-century landscape that would most impress us, were we able to see it now, would be its all-pervading wetness, in highways, fields and woods alike. Now, as a result of more efficient agricultural drainage, most of the countryside is dry for at least the warmer months of the year - too dry, many would say, for the vegetation and wildlife of damp areas has vanished along with the water.

But in the naturally wet country around Frampton itself the changes have been less drastic. In the heart of the 1984 West Country drought there was still standing water in some of the hollows and furrows of the local grazing marshes. Thanks to a combination of local geography and a tradition of respectful husbandry there is as great a variety of watery places as there would have been in the 1840s (more, in fact, since a group of gravel pits, now flooded, were dug in the estate grounds earlier this century). They covered the whole gamut of wetland habitats: the ponds on Frampton Green (linked, remember, with the ornamental canal in Frampton Court, which no doubt meant a free passage of plant seeds between the two sites); the meandering and luxuriantly edged river Frome and the Gloucester and Berkeley canal, opened in 1827; the grazing marshes, already drained and embanked but often flooded in the winter, and the water meadows which were deliberately submerged with fresh water to encourage grass growth; the drainage dikes (known as 'rhines' locally) which had already begun to act as refuges for the plants from the drained marshes: and the river Severn itself, with its range of salt-water habitats (see page 136).

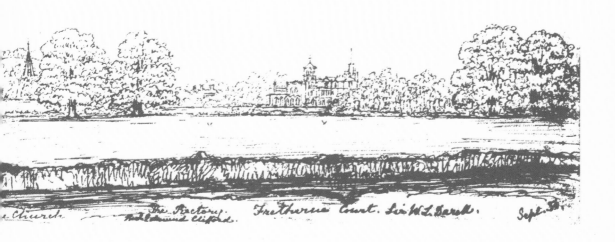

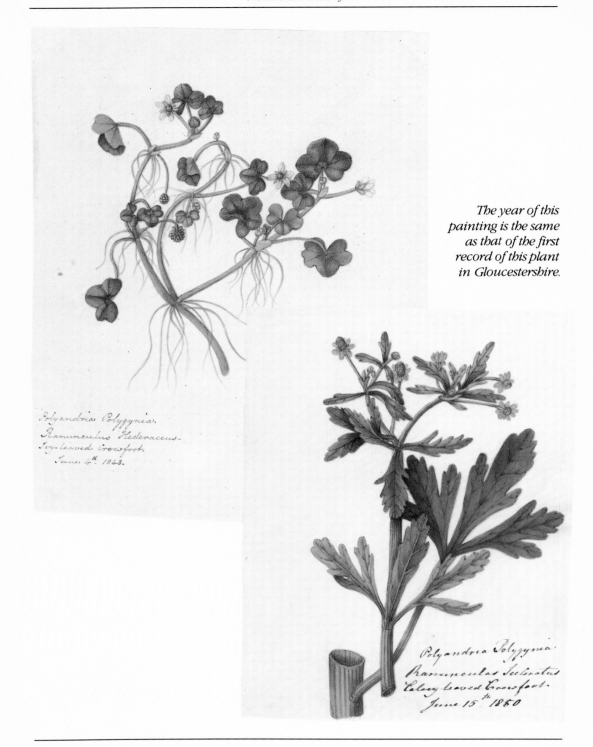

Polyandria Polygynia.
Ranunculus Hederaceus.
Ivy-leaved Crowfoot.
June 4th 1843.

Polyandria Polygynia.
Ranunculus Sceleratus.
Celery leaved Crowfoot.
June 15th 1850

*The year of this
painting is the same
as that of the first
record of this plant
in Gloucestershire.*

Ivy-leaved crowfoot
Ranunculus hederaceus
June 4th 1843
The margins of ponds, shallow streams
and wet pastures. Now rare and
declining

Celery-leaved buttercup
Ranunculus sceleratus
June 15th 1850
Rather common in ditches, slow
streams and ponds

Polyandria Polygynia
Ranunculus Aquatilis & Panthothius
White floating Crowfoot & Small Do —

The water crowfoots are notoriously variable species, and it is hard to be certain of the identities of the two illustrated here. The species on the left is labelled as Ranunculus aquatilis, *now known as common water crowfoot, though it is curious that the artist painted only the underwater foliage and not the more substantial floating leaves.*

The species on the right appears to be fan-leaved water crowfoot, Ranunculus circinatus.

The tangle of underwater leaves - and by extension water crowfoot itself - is known locally by the expressive name of rait.

Water crowfoot species
Ponds, canals, ditches

Tetradynamia Siliquosa
Nasturtium officinale

Common Water Cress
Aug.ᵗ 14ᵗʰ 1850

Watercress
Rorippa nasturtium-aquaticum
August 14th 1850
Streams, ditches
Local name: carpenter's chips

Decandria Pentagynia
Lychnis Flos Cuculi

Ragged Robin Campion
June 1849

Dodecandria Monogynia
Lythrum Salicaria Purple Lythrum
Sept. 5. 1850

Ragged Robin
Lychnis flos-cuculi
June 1849
Damp pastures and meadows.
Widespread but declining

Purple loosestrife
Lythrum salicaria
September 5th 1850
Fairly frequent by rivers and ditches

Monandria Monogynia
Hippuris Vulgaris Common Marestail

Octandria Trigynia
Polygonum Persicaria
Spotted Persicaria

Redshank
Polygonum persicaria
Riverbanks, damp waste places,
woodland rides

Marestail
Hippuris vulgaris
Uncommon in ponds, ditches, and
canals

Monandria Digynia.
Callitriche Verna. — Vernal water Starwort.
June 5th 1843.

Common water starwort
Callitriche stagnalis
June 5th 1843
Ponds, ditches, canals, damp tracks

The winged stems which characterize this species (and which show up well in this painting) made water figwort a popular musical instrument among country children, especially in western Britain. When the stems are scraped together, the wings vibrate and produce a sound not unlike a badly played violin.

Didynamia Angiospermia
Scrophularia aquatica
Water Figwort August 1843

Water figwort
Scrophularia aquatica
August 1843
Ditches, riversides, damp scrub

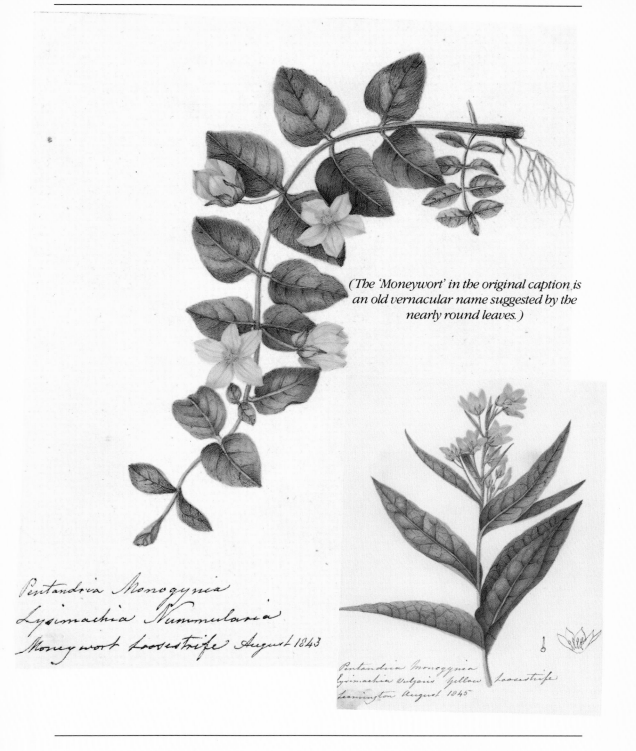

(The 'Moneywort' in the original caption is an old vernacular name suggested by the nearly round leaves.)

Pentandria Monogynia
Lysimachia Nummularia
Moneywort Loosestrife August 1843

Pentandria Monogynia
Lysimachia vulgaris Yellow Loosestrife
Leamington August 1845

Creeping Jenny
Lysimachia nummularia
August 1843
Wet meadows, ditch-edges, damp
woods. Now uncommon and
declining

Yellow loosestrife
Lysimachia vulgaris
August 1845, Leamington
Ditches, fens, river edges. Not
common

Myosotis palustris Water Scorpion Grass   August 1839

Pentandria Monogynia

Diandria Monogynia

Veronica Beccabunga Brooklime Speedwell

June 3rd 1840 Frampton

Brooklime

Veronica beccabunga

June 3rd 1840, Frampton

Ditches, ponds, streams, wet meadows

Water forget-me-not

Myosotis scorpioides

August 1839

Ditches, ponds, stream-sides

Diandria Monogynia

Veronica Anagallis   Water Speedwell

Frampton from pool by Denfurlong Farm
July 11th 1849

Common comfrey
Symphytum officinale
Ditches, stream-sides, wet meadows,
waysides

Water speedwell
Veronica anagallis-aquatica
July 11th 1849, 'Frampton from the
pool by Denfurlong Farm' (a tenant
farm of the Cliffords)
Ditches, streams, ponds. Widespread
but not common

This hybrid between marsh woundwort and hedge woundwort (page 60) was a good find. It is generally rather rare in Gloucestershire and was not recorded for the Frampton area until the early years of this century, when A.D. Norton found it near Coaley, a couple of miles to the south. The hybrid characteristics are brought out well in the painting: the rather coarse habit and leaf-stalks typical of hedge woundwort, with the narrow leaves and pale pink flowers of marsh woundwort.

Stachys ambigua
August 1st 1846, Frampton
Canal banks, pond-sides, hedge-banks.
Scarce

Water mint
Mentha aquatica
September 21st 1849
Ditches, ponds, streams, wet meadows
Local name: horse mint

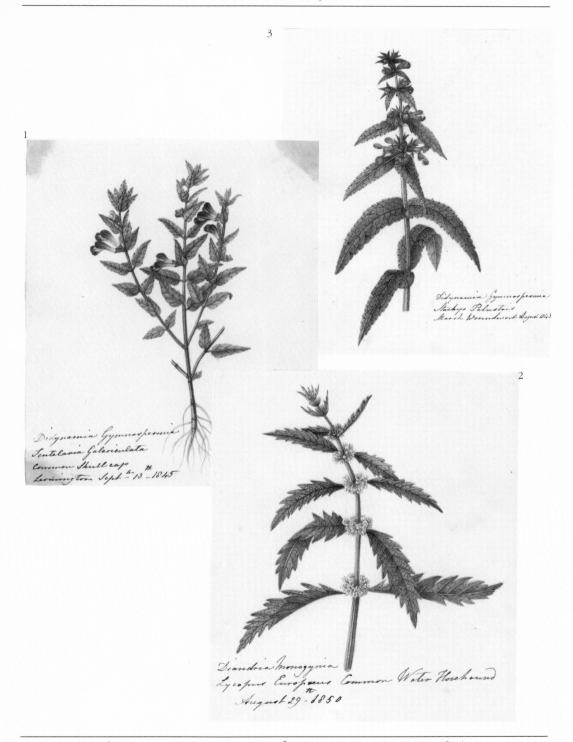

Didynamia Gymnospermia
Stachys Palustris
Marsh Woundwort August 1843

Didynamia Gymnospermia
Scutelaria Galericulata
Common Skullcap
Leamington Sept. 13th 1845

Diandria Monogynia
Lycopus Europaeus Common Water Horehound
August 29th 1850

1	2	3
Skullcap	**Gipsywort**	**Marsh woundwort**
Scutellaria galericulata	*Lycopus europaeus*	*Stachys palustris*
September 13th 1845, Leamington	August 29th 1850	August 1843
Frequent in ditches, by canals and stream-sides	Ditches, ponds, stream-sides	Ditches, riversides, hedge-banks

Syngenesia Polygamia Superflua

Inula Dysenterica Common Fleabane Inula

August 1847

Common fleabane
Pulicaria dysenterica
August 1847
Damp places, pastures, pond edges.
Still occurs on Frampton Green

Tetrandria Tetragynia
Potamogeton crispum Curled Pond Weed
From Fishpond May 1847

Syngenesia Polygamia Superflua
Senecio Aquaticus Marsh Ragwort
Stancombe Augt 8th

Marsh ragwort
Senecio aquaticus
August 8th, Stancombe
Quite common in ditch edges, wet
meadows and pastures

Curled pondweed
Potamogeton crispus
May 1847, 'From fishpond'
(presumably at Frampton Court)
Ponds, streams, canals, ditches

Class 6th · Order 3rd —

Triglochin Palustre
Marsh Arrow Grass 2

Triglochin maritimum Sea Arrow Grass 1

1
Sea arrowgrass
Triglochin maritima
Sea arrowgrass grows in salt-marshes,
and is rather local

2
Marsh arrowgrass
Triglochin palustris
Marsh arrowgrass occurs in wet
meadows and pastures. It is now
uncommon and declining

Triandria Monogynia
Iris Pseudacorus Yellow Iris
June 21st 1845

Butomus Umbellatus
Flowering Rush

Enneandria Monogynia

Although this particular painting was copied, flowering rush would have been familiar to the Cliffords from the ponds and rivers round Frampton. Marianne Phelps recorded it from 'the Stroud canal and the Cambridge brook'.

Flowering rush
Butomus umbellatus
Copied from an illustration in Smith
and Sowerby's *English Botany*
(volume X plate 651 (1800))
Ditches, canals, ponds. Local, and
nowhere common

Yellow iris
Iris pseudacorus
June 21st 1845
Ditches, ponds, stream-sides, wet
pastures

Severn-side

The river Severn is tidal as far as Gloucester and gives Frampton something approaching a shoreline. There is no sand or shingle but there are mudflats, small areas of salt-marsh, sea walls, mud-banks, and brackish creeks. Because of the funnel-like shape of the estuary, the tides can be quite fierce at times. The most regular surge is the famous tidal wave known as the Severn Bore, which tends to be most pronounced in spring and autumn. And, despite the substantial sea walls, there has always been flooding, especially when the estuary is full of fresh water after heavy winter rains or snow-melts. All this activity continually rearranges the river-edge habitats, and keeps them open for maritime plants.

A carefully drawn picture, emphasizing the features which distinguish this species from the similar and almost equally common greater sea spurrey, S. media. (The lesser has sepals slightly longer than the petals, and only slightly shorter than the seed capsule).

Lesser sea spurrey
Spergularia marina
Drier parts of salt-marshes

1
Sea milkwort
Glaux maritima
Salt-marshes

2
Marsh mallow
Althaea officinalis
September 1847
Banks of brackish ditches. Scarce and
local

3
Lesser centaury
Centaurium pulchellum
Sandy places. Very rare.
The first official Gloucestershire
record is not until 1869, and this
picture may be a copy

Tetrandria Monogynia
Plantago Maritima

Sea Plantain
August 1850

Sea plantain
Plantago maritima
August 1850
Muddy tidal banks

Spiny restharrow
Ononis spinosa
'By the Severn'
Sea walls, drier parts of shoreline,
waysides

Monadelphia Polyandria
Lavatera Arborea Sea Tree Mallow
August 16th 1843

Tree mallow
Lavatera arborea
August 16th 1843
Dry banks. Possibly native by the
Severn, but also widely cultivated in
gardens

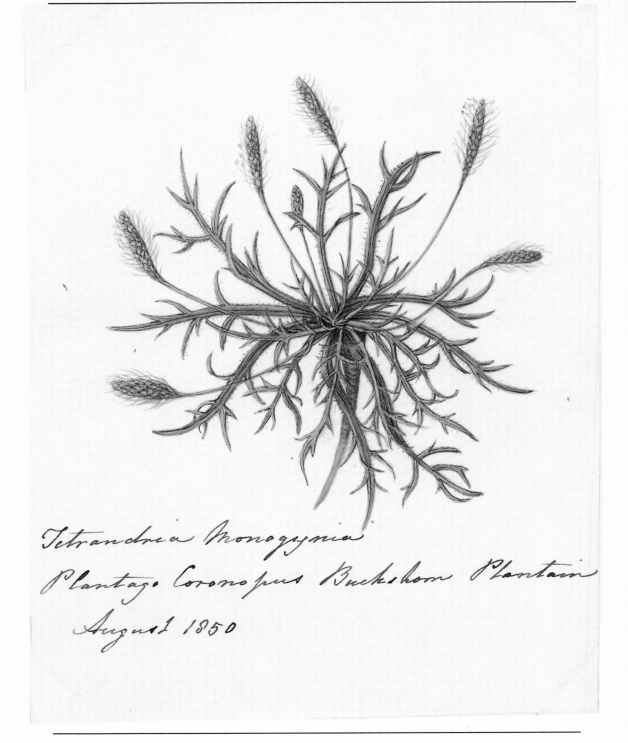

Tetrandria Monogynia

Plantago Coronopus Buckshorn Plantain

August 1850

Buck's-horn plantain
Plantago coronopus
August 1850
Dry, sandy banks

Syngenesia Polygamia Superflua

Aster Tripolium   Sea Aster
or
Starwort

Sea aster
Aster tripolium
Salt-marshes, brackish ditches
Local name: muck-button

Field Weeds

Advances in seed-cleaning techniques and ever more powerful weed-killers have made this the most devastated of all the plant groups in this book. No less than eight of the twenty species illustrated have declined to such an extent since the last war that they appear only on an occasional basis in Gloucestershire. One, the corn cockle, is now a national rarity.

Arable weeds may already have been declining at the time these paintings were being made. Frampton's common fields were enclosed in 1815, and though this may have involved the bringing of some permanent pasture into cultivation (thus increasing the opportunities for weed seeds to germinate) it also laid the foundations for what came to be called 'hygienic agriculture'. Enclosure meant the end of the unploughed baulks between individual strips in the common field and a reduction in the size of the headlands. And by rationalizing the holdings it opened the way for new agricultural technology, and in particular the mechanical drill, which sowed seed in straight evenly spaced rows and facilited much easier hoeing of weeds.

The viciously spiny seed-heads of the corn buttercup gave it one of the nastiest collections of local names of any British plant - including clench, devil's claws, devil-on-all-sides, devil-on-both-sides, devil's coachwheel, devil's currycomb and hellweed but no names exclusive to Gloucestershire have been recorded.

One of the most attractive of cornfield weeds, pheasant's eye was once so plentiful in cultivated areas on the chalk soils of southern England that it was gathered and sent to Covent Garden Market, where it was sold under the name of 'red morocco'.

Polyandria Polygnia
Adonis autumnalis
Corn Pheasant's Eye
Oct. 10th 1848

Corn buttercup
Ranunculus arvensis
June 1847, 'From Cornfield towards
Whitminster'
Arable fields, waste ground. Now
scarce

Pheasant's eye
Adonis annua
October 10th 1848
Arable fields, waste ground, gardens.
Now very scarce
Local name: love lies bleeding

Polyandria monogynia
Papaver Rhoeas Common red Poppy
July 1847

The alternative names of corn poppy and field poppy make clear the old association of the plant with cornfields though, since the First World War, the red flower has also been used as a symbol of those who died in the fields of Flanders or on later battlefields

A 'Surfeit Water' from the Frampton domestic recipe book: 'Pick Poppies clean from the stalks, with a chopping knife cut them small. Put ½ 1b of poppies to a Gallon of boiling water. Let it stand 24 hours. Then press it thro' a hair bag. Put the liquor into a cask and to every Gallon wine measure put ½ 1b of good Lisbon sugar. It will ferment, and as soon as the fermentation ceases, it is fit for the still.'

Common poppy
Papaver rhoeas
July 1847
Fields, waysides, waste ground
Local name: popple

Diadelphia Hexandria 1st
Fumaria Parviflora Small flowered Fumitory
July 12th 1845

Common fumitory
Fumaria officinalis
July 12th 1845
Fields, waste places, gardens

Wild candytuft
Iberis amara
Catherine Elizabeth Clifford
Cornfields, chalk downs, waste
ground. Now scarce

Tetradynamia Siliquosa.
Sinapis Arvensis
Charlock Mustard
June 1849

Charlock
Sinapis arvensis
June 1849
Fields and waste places
Local names: cadlock, carlock, calves'
feet

Decandria Pentagynia

Agrostemma Githago

Corn Cockle

Arable fields. Now almost certainly extinct in Gloucestershire and a nationally rare species, with records from only four British locations since 1960.

A magnificent painting, probably by Mary Anne Clifford. It catches perfectly the jizz of the flower, the occasional asymmetry of the petals and the way they are scrolled or furled like a flag just before opening.

Corn cockle

Agrostemma githago
Local name: cockleford

This is an unusual variety of the small-flowered catchfly, *Silene gallica*, which has occasionally been cultivated as an ornamental plant. It occurs as a very rare casual in cultivated ground and has been recorded on the banks of the Severn near Gloucester docks.

Variegated catchfly
Silene quinquevulnera
July 13th 1843

Corn spurrey
Spergula arvensis
Leamington
Cultivated fields on light sandy soils.
Rare

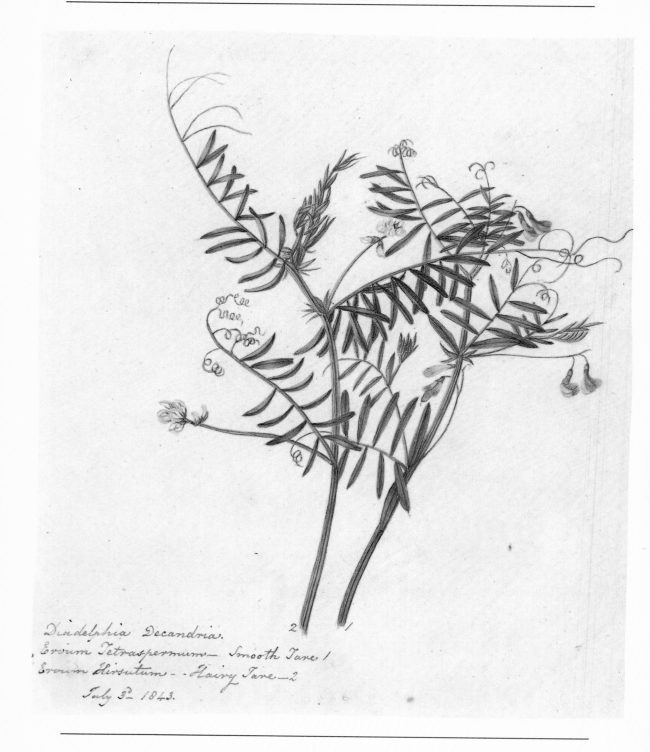

Diadelphia Decandria.
Ervum Tetraspermum — Smooth Tare 1
Ervum Hirsutum - Hairy Tare — 2
July 3ᵈ 1843.

Smooth tare and Hairy tare
Vicia tetrasperma and Vicia hirsuta
July 3rd 1843
Cultivated fields, waysides

Shepherd's needle was regarded as common throughout the wheat-growing areas of England even into the early 1960s. Since then it has suffered a catastrophic decline and would have to be regarded not only as rare but occasional in Gloucestershire. This specimen was found about half a mile from Frampton, in 'a cornfield on the way to Whitminster'. (Corn buttercup is captioned with the same location and the same date, and it's probable the two were painted in the same field.)

It is an evocative, airy picture, painted in midsummer when the long seed-pods that give the species its name would have been ripening. It is also the only umbellifer painted by the Cliffords, and it may be no coincidence that an exception was made for a plant whose fruits were considerably more interesting and conspicuous than its nondescript white flowers.

The group of seeds in the foregound have been splayed and slightly exaggerated in size for emphasis, and perhaps to bring out what Gerard had noticed two hundred and fifty years earlier, that they resembled 'pack needles, orderlie set one by another, like the great teeth of a combe'.

Pentandria Digynia
Scandix Pecten-veneris
Common Shepherd's needle June 1847
From Corn Field on the way to Whitminster

Shepherd's needle
Scandix pecten-veneris
June 1847, 'From Cornfield on the way
to Whitminster'
Arable fields, especially on chalky soils.
Now rare and declining

Anagallis Pimpernel

Pentandria Monogynia Frampton July 1838

*The blue flowers featured in the painting are
an occasional colour variant.*

1	2	3	4
Field forget-me-not	**Small nettle**	**Black nightshade**	**Scarlet pimpernel**
Myosotis arvensis	*Urtica urens*	*Solanum nigrum*	*Anagallis arvensis*
June 1847	Fields and gardens on light soils.	October 1844	July 1838, Frampton
Cultivated and waste land	Infrequent	Cultivated land, manure heaps, waste ground	Dry, cultivated and waste ground. Local name: shepherd's clock (from the habit of the flowers of shutting in dull weather)

Pentandria Monogynia
Convolvulus arvensis
Small Bindweed
July 24th 1848

Field bindweed
Convolvulus arvensis
July 24th 1848
Cultivated ground, waysides, waste
land

Didynamia Angiospermia
Antirrhinum Spuria Round-leaved Toadflax
August 22nd 1848

This is an interestingly early record for this uncommon and inconspicuous cornfield weed. The *Flora of Gloucestershire* gives its first county record as 1830, but it was not officially recorded from Frampton itself until A.D. Norton found it there in the 1930s.

Round-leaved fluellen
Kickxia spuria
August 22nd 1848
Cornfields, especially on lime-rich
soils. Now rare and declining

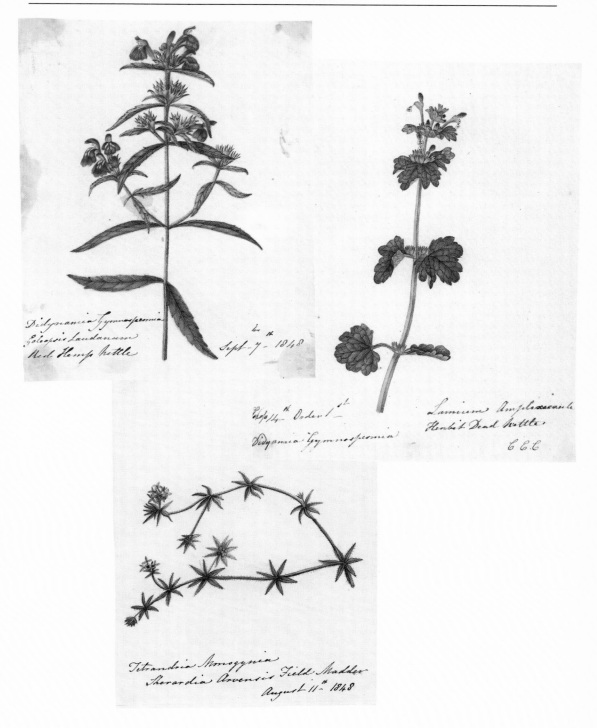

1	2	3
Red hemp-nettle	**Field madder**	**Henbit dead-nettle**
Galeopsis angustifolia	*Sherardia arvensis*	*Lamium amplexicaule*
September 7th 1848	August 11th 1848	Catherine Elizabeth Clifford
Cornfields on lime-rich soils, and waste ground. Scarce and declining	Cornfields on lime-rich soils, bare downland. Declining	Cultivated fields, waste land, gardens

The Colonists

There is one final group of 'wild' plants that is difficult to classify: those species, native in other parts of the world, that have become naturalized close to human habitation. Sometimes these are garden escapes, sometimes accidental introductions with foreign imports of grain or fleeces. The Severn Vale was especially rich in aliens because of its string of ports, and Bristol and Gloucester docks have some of the highest scores for stowaway plants of any cities in Britain.

Decandria Digynia
Saponaria Officinalis
Common Soapwort October 16th 1848

Soapwort

Saponaria officinalis
October 16th 1848. (Copied from
Smith and Sowerby's *English Botany*
(volume XV plate 1060 (1802))
Waste ground and waysides near
habitation. Possibly native, but in most
sites an escape from gardens

Pentandria Monogynia
Pulmonaria Officinalis Common Lungwort
April 2nd 1846 Frampton

Lungwort
Pulmonaria officinalis
April 2nd 1846, Frampton
Shady places, churchyards,
hedge-banks near houses.
Garden escape from Europe

Rose of Sharon
Hypericum calycinum
August 14th 1849, Stancombe
Shady banks, shrubberies near houses.
Garden escape from south-east
Europe

Octandria Trigynia
Persicaria Fagopyrum
Buckwheat Persicaria
Sept. 26 - 1850

Didynamia Gymnospermia
Teucrium Chamaedrys Woll Germander

Buckwheat

Fagopyrum esculentum
September 26th 1850
Waste and cultivated ground.
Occasional introduction with grain,
bird seed, etc. Introduced from Asia
originally

Wall germander

Teucrium chamaedrys
Walls, rocky places. Garden escape
from southern Europe

Pentandria Monogynia
Polemonium Caerulium Blue Jacob's Ladder 1847

It is pleasantly appropriate that Jacob's ladder should crop up on stony waysides and rubbish tips, since it was one of the first plants to recolonize the disturbed rocky ground left behind in the wake of the last glaciers.

Jacob's ladder

Polemonium caeruleum
Waste ground. Native in limestone
areas of northern Britain, but
elsewhere invariably a garden escape

Pentandria Monogynia   *Hyoscyamus, Henbane*
Frampton August 7th 1838

Henbane
Hyoscyamus niger
August 7th 1838, Frampton
Waste and cultivated ground. Sandy and
gravelly areas near the sea. A relict of old herb
gardens, and an occasional impurity in clover
seed imported from central Europe

A fiercely narcotic plant whose history is every bit as sinister as this brooding picture suggests. Dr Crippen used it as one of his poisons. In the seventeenth and eighteenth centuries herbalists employed it against the toothache, because of a certain resemblance between henbane's seed-pods and a row of decrepit molars. The sufferers were not only doped by this potent drug, but often duped as well, as John Gerard relates:

'The seed is used of mountibancke toothdrawers which runne about the countrey, for to cause woormes come foorth of mens teeth by burning it in a chafing-dish with coles, the partie holding his mouth over the fume thereof: but some craftie companions to gaine money convey small lute strings into the water, perswading the patient that those small creeping beasts came out of his mouth or other parts which he intended to ease.'

These days henbane is still grown commercially to provide the sedative drugs hyoscine and atropine, and very occasionally, naturalized specimens may originate with bird-sown seeds from one of these plots. But most come over as impurities in red clover seed from central Europe or spring from long-buried seeds in obsolete herb gardens. Henbane's seeds have a proven dormancy period of at least a hundred years. The Cliffords' specimen probably sprang up in a particularly hot summer, either in part of their own garden or down on the Severn shoreline.

Yellow corydalis
Corydalis lutea
Walls and roofs. Garden escape from
southern Europe

Entrance Gate to Frampton Court

Gardens

It is harder to reconstruct the details and plantings of the Clifford gardens than those of any of the other habitats. Both at Frampton and Stancombe they have been remodelled and replanted many times. The features that do survive suggest somewhat elaborate layouts in the English landscape style. As well as its splendid ornamental canal, Frampton had fine lawns and tree-lined drives, conservatories, and a walled garden whose bricks were made from salty clay dug from a marshland quarry on the estate. Stancombe had a lake and a number of grottos and follies.

As for the flowers, the following pages give an idea of what may have been the Cliffords favourites. The varieties of pansies and pelargoniums, both rather new and fashionable plants in the first half of the nineteenth century, suggest that they kept well abreast of contemporary trends in horticulture.

The garden-flower paintings are almost exclusively by the older generation of Cliffords, and the majority were probably done from specimens in Charlotte Anne's extensive grounds at Stancombe Park.

C. Clifford – Nov 19th /42

Strawberry tree
Arbutus unedo
Native in western Ireland and popular
in nineteenth-century gardens.
Flowers in autumn, while the previous
year's berries are still ripening

Laurustinus
Viburnum tinus
A favourite winter-flowering evergreen

Alba rose
Possibly 'Maiden's Blush'

The yuccas are natives of southern North America and the West Indies, but at least one species was cultivated in England early in the seventeenth century.

Yucca species

Introduced to gardens from southern
Europe in the sixteenth century, originally as
a medicinal plant. (Its pods were used as a
mild substitute for senna.)

Euphorbia mellifera
A shrubby euphorbia native to Madeira

Bladder senna
Colutea arborescens

Dodecandria Dodecagynia
Sempervivum tectorum
Common House-leek
July 20th 1850

Houseleek
Sempervivum tectorum
July 20th 1850

The ancestors of our garden fuchsias were
brought to this country (chiefly from South
America) in the 1830s, and became
popular with florists from 1840.

Fuchsia species

A Frampton Pomona

Fruit-growing was once widespread in Gloucestershire. On early nineteenth-century maps, there are orchards marked throughout the parish, including a number inside the grounds of Frampton Court itself. Espaliered fruit-trees were also grown against the salty bricks of the Court's walled gardens.

Now, with the mechanization and centralization of fruit-growing, most of these local orchards have vanished, grubbed out or allowed to become derelict. The huge circular stones that once pressed the cider apples from the Frampton estate now prop up rockery plants in the lawns.

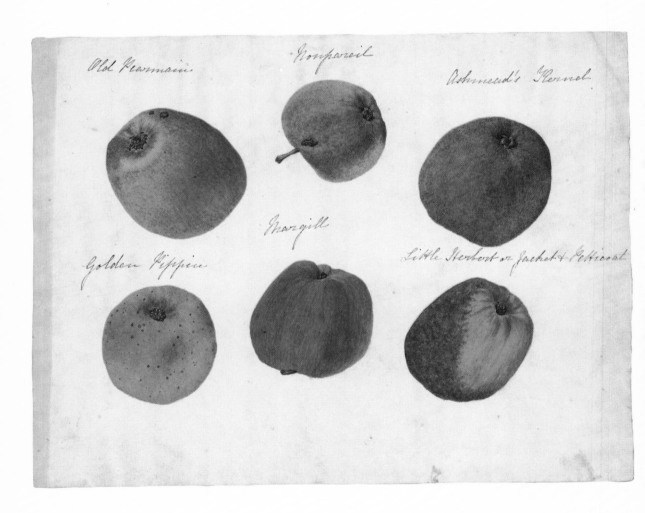

The decline in small-scale local fruit growing has been accompanied by a vast contraction in the number of varieties of fruit which are available commercially. Of the dozen varieties of apple painted here, only two or three still appear in shops. Three, Golden Rennett (or Reinette), Golden Pippin and Non-Pareil go back to at least the sixteenth century. Two others are distinctly local apples, and the varieties shown here may well be those that grew in the Cliffords' own orchards. Little Herbert, or Jacket and Petticoat was first noted in the county in 1851, and Ashmead's Kernel was raised by Dr Ashmead in Gloucester in 1720. Over a century later Robert Hogg wrote that 'it has long been a favourite apple in all the gardens of West Gloucestershire, but it does not seem to have been known in other parts of the country. Like the Ribston Pippin it appears to have remained long in obscurity, before its value was generally appreciated.' It is still not as well known as it might be, although it continues to be grown and recently seems to have been spreading a little from Gloucestershire.

Although a quince jelly may be made from
its fruit, this shrub, better known as
japonica, is usually grown for the sake of its
flowers

Pyrus Japonica.
C.C. May 2nd/63

Japanese quince
Chaenomeles japonica
May 2nd 1863, Charlotte Clifford

Orchard trees are probably the commonest site for mistletoe in the area. In a survey in neighbouring Herefordshire in the 1860s, Dr G.H. Bull recorded the species on 34 per cent of all apple trees.

In her annotations in Baxter, Marianne Phelps records mistletoe as occurring on sycamore, almond, acacia (presumably *Robinia*), rose, plane, willow, poplar and an 'Oak near Frampton'.

Mistletoe
Viscum album
February 1849

This fine collection of pansies, on the right, demonstrates more than any other picture how adventurous the Cliffords and Purnells were as gardeners. The very first cultivated pansies had been developed just twenty-five years earlier, by William Thompson and William Richardson, gardeners respectively to Lord Gambier at Iver and Lady Bennett at Walton-on-Thames. Richardson's work was chiefly concerned with selecting interesting sports and hybrids from among the very variable populations of our little native heartsease, Viola tricolor. *By the 1820s he had managed to raise some twenty new varieties from this source alone.*

Meanwhile Thompson was working with one of our other native pansies, the mountain pansy, Viola lutea. *As well as the obvious advantages of being a perennial (it was hardy, and could be propagated by cuttings) it had a more compact habit than* V. tricolor *and held its flowers on more upright stalks. Selections from seedlings and varieties of this species increased the range of cultivars still further. There was also a certain amount of accidental crossing (by insect cross-pollination) between the cultivars, and maybe even with the heartsease.*

Snowbell
Soldanella montana
Already a popular alpine

Auricula
Primula auricula
cultivar

Soon there were more than two hundred varieties in private collections, and by the end of the decade they were in limited circulation among enthusiasts, selling for between 1s and 4s a plant. In 1841 the first Pansy Society was formed, and just one year later the artist, Rosamond Clifford, was able to paint this impressive collection of a flower most of whose old varieties are now, sadly, extinct.

The four varieties at the top of the painting show clearly the narrow 'face' and long stalks associated with their mountain pansy parentage. (In fact, they are more like what we now call bedding violas, though strictly speaking these were not brought into existence until the 1860s when the very upright, alpine Viola cornuta *was brought into the breeding line.) Bottom left is an example of the kind of pansy bred for show, where the aim was to produce as nearly circular a flower as possible.*

Florist's pansies
Viola cultivars
June 11th 1842, Stancombe,
Rosamond Clifford

Pelargonium
(Charlotte Anne Purnell?)

This collection of pelargoniums demonstrates the contrasting styles of at least three of the family: Charlotte Clifford, Rosamond Clifford, Marianne Phelps (later Marianne Clifford) and probably Charlotte Anne Purnell.

Pelargonium
July 10th 1848, Charlotte Clifford

Pelargonium
1837, Marianne Phelps

Scented-leaved, pot and zonal pelargoniums, as the various kinds were called, were brought to this country from the Cape in the late seventeenth century. They became something of a vogue in the mid-nineteenth century, following the rise in popularity of the hothouses and conservatories in which they needed to be overwintered.

Pelargonium
1840, Rosamond Clifford

Garden phlox
Phlox paniculata cultivar
Charlotte Anne Purnell
(Not in her usual signature)

Hyacinth

Hyacinthus orientalis cultivar
This hyacinth is the most strikingly
stylized and modern of all Charlotte
Anne Purnell's paintings

2

Rosamond Clifford
Frampton March 15th - 1839.

3

1

March 1839 R.C.

1	2	3
Cyclamen	**Snowdrop**	**Crocus** cultivars
Cyclamen hederifolium	*Galanthus nivalis*	March 1839, Rosamond Clifford
May 19th 1845, Charlotte Clifford	March 25th 1839, Rosamond Clifford	
	A nearly double garden variety	

Alexandria Monogynia

Convallaria Multiflora Solomon's Seal Common

May 1843

Although this native species does occur in limestone areas in England it is very rare in the southern Cotswolds (where it is replaced by angular Solomon's Seal, *P. odoratum*) and this painting was probably made from a garden specimen.

Solomon's seal
Polygonatum multiflorum

Some of the striking annual flowers that were beginning to become popular in the early nineteenth century.

Californian bluebell
Phacelia campanularia

Dwarf morning glory
Convolvulus minor
August 9th 1842, Rosamond Clifford

Baby blue eyes
Nemophila insignis
Brought to this country from America
in the 1820s by the young
plant-collector David Douglas

Stocks
Matthiola incana cultivars

The winged stems and rather small clusters of dull maroon and grey flowers suggest that this specimen was not far removed from the wild sweet pea of southern Italy. In fact our modern sweet peas did not really begin to be developed until after 1850. Most of the breeders were amateurs, and many were clergymen. In 1900, a country parson gave an address on the bicentenary of the arrrival of the sweet pea in this country that would have endeared him to an earlier generation of Cliffords (see page 75): 'Gentlemen, the sweet pea has a keel that was meant to seek all shores. It has wings that were meant to fly across all continents. It has a standard which is friendly to all nations. It has a fragrance like the universal gospel.'

Sweet pea
Lathyrus odoratus cultivar
Rosamond Clifford

Bibliography

ALLEN, David Elliston. *The Naturalist in Britain: a Social History.* London, 1976.

BARBER, Lynn. *The Heyday of Natural History.* London, 1980.

BAXTER, William. *British Phaenogamous Botany; or, Figures and Descriptions of the Genera of British Flowering Plants.* 6 volumes. Oxford, 1833-43.

BLUNT, Wilfrid. *The Art of Botanical Illustration.* London, 1950.

BLUNT, Wilfrid, and RAPHAEL, Sandra. *The Illustrated Herbal.* London, 1979.

BRITTEN, J., and HOLLAND, R. *Dictionary of English Plant-names.* London, 1878-86.

CLAPHAM, A. R., TUTIN, T. G., and WARBURG, E. F. *Flora of the British Isles.* Second edition. Cambridge, 1962.

DONY, J. G., ROB, C. M., and PERRING, F. H. *English Names of Wild Flowers.* London, 1974.

DUNN, S. T. *Alien Flora of Britain.* London, 1905.

EASTWOOD, Dorothea. 'Young Ladies and Old Botany Books' in *Mirror of Flowers.* London, 1953.

FISHER, John. *The Origins of Garden Plants.* London, 1982.

GERARD, John. *The Herball.* London 1597. Facsimile, Amsterdam, 1974. Second edition, enlarged and amended by Thomas Johnson. London, 1633. Facsimile, New York, 1975.

GLOUCESTERSHIRE RECORD OFFICE. *Gloucestershire Turnpike Roads.* 1976. *Gloucestershire Waterways.* 1977. *Inclosure in Gloucestershire.* 1976.

GRIGSON, Geoffrey. *The Englishman's Flora.* London, 1958.

HOGG, Robert. *The Fruit Manual.* Fifth edition. London, 1884.

KNAPP, J. L. *Journal of a Naturalist.* London, 1829.

LOUSLEY, J. E. *Wild flowers of Chalk and Limestone.* London, 1969.

ORDNANCE SURVEY. First edition series, reprinted. Newton Abbot, 1968.

PERRING, F. H., and FARRELL, L. *British Red Data Books 1: Vascular Plants.* Nettlesham, 1977.

PERRING, F. H., and WALTERS, S. M. *Atlas of the British Flora.* London, 1962. Second edition. East Ardsley, 1977.

PEVSNER, Nikolaus. *The Leaves of Southwell.* Harmondsworth, 1945.

RIDDELSDELL, H. J., HEDLEY, G. W., and PRICE, W. R. *Flora of Gloucestershire.* Cheltenham, 1948.

SALISBURY, Edward. *Weeds and Aliens.* London, 1964.

SCOTT-JAMES, Anne. *The Cottage Garden.* London, 1981.

SMITH, A. H. *The Place-names of Gloucestershire.* Cambridge, 1964-65.

SMITH, James Edward, and SOWERBY, James. *English Botany.* 36 volumes. London, 1790-1814. Second edition, arranged according to the Linnaean method; with the descriptions shortened, and occasional remarks by Charles Johnson. 12 volumes. London, 1831-46.

WITHERING, William. *An Arrangement of British Plants.* Seventh edition. 4 volumes. London 1830.

Index